CASES IN FINANCE

Cases in Finance

Frederick C. Scherr
West Virginia University

Macmillan Publishing Company
New York

Collier Macmillan Publishers
London

Macmillan Publishing Company
866 Third Avenue, New York, New York 10022

Collier Macmillan Canada, Inc.

Library of Congress Cataloging in Publication Data

Scherr, Frederick C.
  Cases in finance.

  1. Corporations—Finance—Case studies. I. Title.
HG4015.5.S32 1984   658.1'5   83-1024
ISBN 0-02-406780-6

Printing: 1 2 3 4 5 6 7 8   Year: 4 5 6 7 8 9 0 1 2

ISBN 0-02-406780-6

To Tom and Ellen

PREFACE

In the world of practicing financial managers, decisions are often more complicated than problems presented in introductory finance texts. Managers face situations in which extraneous arguments and data are available but critical data are often missing. To deal with such situations, they must identify the type of decision to be made, separate the useful data from the extraneous, and make forecasts and assumptions to generate critical missing data.

Cases, to my thinking, provide a bridge between the world of the textbook and the world of the practicing financial manager. Cases challenge the student to perform, in an abridged context, the tasks required of an on-line financial decision maker; they simulate the real world.

This casebook contains forty-four cases in financial management. It is intended for use with relatively large undergraduate classes (twenty-five or more students) at state universities and colleges. The cases can be used as in-class examples or as case problems in conjunction with a first or second course in financial management. At West Virginia University, we use these cases in conjunction with our second financial management course for finance majors. About eighteen cases are used each term. Outlines for several applications are presented in the Instructor's Manual. All cases included here have been used in this fashion. In developing this casebook I have explicitly incorporated a relatively large number involving the management of current assets. The inflation and interest rates of the 1970s and early 1980s have increased concern regarding the management of these investments, and after graduation many undergraduates are likely to be involved initially with current assets management.

Cases included here come from several sources. Some come from my business experience. Some were suggested by financial executives of my acquaintance. Some are based on publicly available materials. Others were contributed by professors or former students. I express my gratitude to all contributors; to the students of West Virginia University, who provided valuable feedback on earlier versions of the cases; and to Chip Price at Macmillan.

F. C. S.

CONTENTS

CASES IN FINANCE

PART I

Financial Analysis

CASE 1

DeWitt-Church Consultants*

Taxation and Business Form

Harold DeWitt was an Assistant Professor of Marketing at a major university. He held an undergraduate degree in sociology, an M.B.A. and a Ph.D. in business administration. Before going back to school to complete his Ph.D., he had worked as a salesman and sales manager for several firms. At the university where Dr. DeWitt taught, a major promotion criteria was the volume of a professor's published works. Scholarly articles in research journals carried the most weight in the promotion review process, and articles in trade journals involving the popularization of academic theories and findings scored some points.

In early 1980, DeWitt was looking through the catalog of extension courses offered by the university. Such courses were held in the evenings for nominal tuition and primarily for adults. One of the courses offered was in the management of on-the-job stress. The course was taught by Rhonda Church, an employee of a local mental health organization, and was co-sponsored by that organization. Ms. Church held undergraduate and Master's degrees in psychology. Problems related to on-the-job stress had recently been the topic of articles in several business magazines and newspapers. Because he perceived this to be a "hot" topic, Dr. DeWitt telephoned Ms. Church to propose that they co-author one or more articles on techniques in the

*This case was co-authored by Dr. Adolph Neidermeyer, Professor of Accounting, West Virginia University.

3

management of on-the-job stress for salesmen. Ms. Church was to provide the expertise on job stress and its management and Dr. DeWitt was to interpret this within the context of salesmanship and sales management. Ms. Church agreed to the proposal, and the two wrote a series of three articles on the topic for a sales trade journal.

Dr. DeWitt and Ms. Church were invited to speak for a fee at the convention of a large sales association. The presentation, which was based on their articles, was well received and sales managers in attendance expressed interest in having the two make similar presentations for firms and local trade organizations. Dr. DeWitt and Ms. Church decided to form a small business, DeWitt-Church Consultants, to handle such presentations. They did not expect these presentations to interfere with their regular jobs, as Ms. Church worked part-time only and Dr. DeWitt had considerable freedom in his schedule. A major concern, however, was how the business should be organized from a legal standpoint. The alternatives were three: partnership, regular incorporation, or Subchapter S incorporation. Because under current statutes no incorporation would limit the liability of such a professional organization and because neither participant saw any possibility of the need for raising outside funds for investment in the business, the decision regarding legal business organization seemed to rest on relative taxation.

Because the material that gave rise to the consultation business was quite topical, Dr. DeWitt and Ms. Church estimated that demand for the service would decrease somewhat in future years. Consequently, they decided on a two-year time horizon and estimated that the business would net, after business-related expenses, about $25,000 during the first year (1981) and $20,000 the second year (1982). The net from the business was to be evenly divided between the two participants. Each planned to save up to one half of their gross before taxes from the business for retirement, if it was possible to shield this amount for federal taxes, and to spend the rest. Dr. DeWitt was married with no children, rented an apartment, and consequently had few federal income tax deductions. He filed the short form and expected his income other than that from the consulting business to be $30,000 in 1981 and $32,000 in 1982. His wife did not work outside the home for income. Ms. Church was married and had one child. Her husband had a responsible job in the banking industry, and together they expected their income for 1981 and 1982 outside of that from the consulting business to be $40,000 per year ($25,000 for Mr. Church and $15,000 for Ms. Church). They owned a home and expected to have itemized deductions of $4,000 in excess of the zero bracket amount (standard deduction amount); they itemized deductions for tax purposes. Some federal income tax rates are presented in Exhibit 1-1.

Some information on the taxation of retirement accounts is appropriate. Most retirement plans, including those considered by Dr. DeWitt and Ms. Church, involve deferring taxes on income until after retirement, at which time one is presumed to be in a lower tax bracket. The simplest of these plans is the individual retirement account (IRA). Any single individual who earns more than $2,000 per year can set up one of these and contribute up to $2,000 per year. For married couples, if only one spouse works for income and makes more than $2,250, the couple may contribute up to $2,250 to such a plan; if both work and both earn more than $2,000, they may contribute up to $4,000 as a couple. The amount contributed is personally

Exhibit 1-1. DEWITT—CHURCH CONSULTANTS

Personal Federal Income Tax Rates for 1981*

Taxable Income[+]		Tax Liability	
Over (1)	Not Over (2)	Base Tax (3)	Per cent of Excess over Column (1) (4)
$ 3,400	$ 5,500	$ 0	14
5,500	7,600	294	16
7,600	11,900	630	18
11,900	16,000	1,404	21
16,000	20,200	2,265	24
20,000	24,600	3,273	28
24,600	29,900	4,505	32
29,900	35,200	6,201	37
35,200	45,800	8,162	43
45,800	60,000	12,720	49
60,000	85,600	19,678	54
85,600	109,400	33,502	59
109,400	162,400	47,544	64
162,400	215,400	81,464	68
215,400	and over	117,504	70

*Source: *Revenue Act of 1978* (Washington, D.C.: Government Printing Office, 1978). Table is for married couples filing joint returns; it does not include tax reductions resulting from the Economic Recovery Act of 1981.

[+]Gross income (if earned) less personal deductions and less standard deductions or itemized deductions.

tax-deductible. Prior to the consulting business, neither of the two participants' family units were investing in IRAs. If either of the corporate forms were adopted, tax-qualified pension plans through the corporation could also be developed, but the corporate deductible contributions to these plans would be limited to 15 per cent of the compensation paid by the corporation to DeWitt or Church during a year, or $7,500, whichever was less.

QUESTIONS

1. Calculate the income and the amount of tax-shielded retirement funds from the consulting business for the family units of Dr. DeWitt and Ms. Church for 1981 and 1982 for each alternative business form of the consulting business. You may make several initial assumptions:
   a. Each will save for retirement the maximum that can be tax shielded up to one-half of their income from the consulting business.
   b. State and local income taxes are trivial.
   c. Incorporation expenses are trivial (note that if this were not so, there would be an initial incorporation expense and noncash write offs in 1981 and 1982). You may also ignore the costs of setting up corporate pension plans.
   d. Use tax rates in Table 1-1; ignore Economic Recovery Act of 1981 adjustments.
   e. If the straight corporate form (non-Subchapter S) is adopted, "reasonable" salaries would be sufficiently high that DeWitt and Church can pay themselves all remaining revenues after corporate pension contributions without the Internal Revenue Service (IRS) questioning such deductions.
   f. All income of both family units is "earned" for tax purposes.

Note that if either corporate form is adopted, IRAs can still be utilized in addition to the corporate pension plan. Present and substantiate a recommendation as to which legal business form should be adopted.

2. If the regular corporate form is adopted, salary deductions to owner-employees for federal corporate income tax purposes are limited to those considered "reasonable" by the IRS. Rework the appropriate parts of your response to Question 1 under the assumption that the IRS will allow tax deductions of only $5,000 per year each for salaries to DeWitt and Church,

and that all business earnings after taxes, if the straight corporate form is adopted, will be paid out in dividends.

3. (At option of the instructor.) Discuss the effect of the dividend taxation policy, as illustrated in Question 2, on the dividend payout decisions of corporations.

Razzle-Dazzle Roofing Company

Ratio Analysis: Investments

Carl Williams was a successful executive with a large firm in Pittsburgh, Pennsylvania. He was in the peak of his earning years and had substantial investments in bonds and stocks. He was seeking an investment with a high potential for long-term capital gains. Williams knew that such an investment would probably also entail significantly greater risks than his other investments, but because he was in a position to replace the capital and intended to limit his investment to $10,000, he was not extremely concerned about this risk. Consequently, when Edward Solomon, his banker, brought up the possibility in early 1980 of investing in a small but growing local business, Williams had been quite interested.

"John Rollins and Jim Dumont founded their roofing firm about five years ago," Solomon had said, "and they have been fairly successful. Both men are in their mid-twenties and are experienced roofers, but not experienced managers. They originally were going to call the firm R and D Roofers but decided to call it Razzle-Dazzle because they thought the name had more appeal. Four years ago, they bought a truck and came to my bank for financing; they also have their checking account with us. Recently, they had problems with bouncing checks and not making payments on the truck. They came to me two weeks ago and explained that they needed additional long-term capital to finance their growth. They wanted to take out a term loan and guarantee it personally. I pointed out that if they are to continue to grow, they will need more financing in the future, not less, and therefore should probably look to some more permanent means of financing. One way to do this, of course, would be to find a private investor such as yourself to buy stock in the firm. I proposed this to John and Jim and they thought it was a good idea. They asked me to bring up the idea to any investors, particularly those who, like yourself, would be classified by the government as minorities. It seems that they do a lot of business with the government in addition to their residential business, and they believe that some minority participation would be beneficial in gaining future business in this area. They gave me permission to show any potential investors their financial statements, which are prepared by a local C.P.A., and a report from a local consultant. I'm afraid the latter isn't very favorable. You'll probably want to review this material and get in touch with John and Jim directly."

As Solomon had suggested, Williams had not found the consultant's report to be very positive. When Rollins and Dumont had started the business five years ago, they had been doing almost all the work themselves and advertising had been strictly by word-of-mouth. Over the years, as the sales of the business had grown, so had the work force, assets, and advertising method. In 1976, the firm bought a truck and took out a loan to finance it. In 1977, the firm had hired two additional full-time workers, rented an office (previously business had been done out of Rollins' home), and bought office furniture. In 1978, the firm incorporated and started to advertise in the yellow pages and in newspapers. In early 1979, the firm had leased a company car.

On the basis of the consultant's report, Williams decided that the consultant's criticisms of the firm centered on three areas: (1) the assets the firm had acquired and how they were being utilized, (2) the type of jobs the firm was taking on and their financing, and (3) how jobs were priced. In the first area, the consultant had particularly objected to the leasing of the company car, a new El Dorado with air conditioning, leather interior, and push-button windows. Lease payments on the car were high, and the consultant claimed that a more useful asset would have been another truck. As of 1979, the firm was working on more than one job but had only one truck; therefore, delays sometimes occurred in getting men and materials to job sites. In the second area, the firm was accepting more and more jobs from state and local government. These jobs were moderately profitable, but the public agencies involved took longer to pay bills than did other accounts. As a result, the company often did not have the cash to pay bills as they came due. Rollins and Dumont, who were good roofers but short on business training and experience, hadn't understood how this could occur. Third, the consultant claimed that Razzle-Dazzle's prices were too low. To the costs of direct labor and direct materials, the firm added a 50 per cent markup in bidding for a job to cover fixed costs and profit. The consultant had claimed that this was too low, considering the new fixed costs the company had undertaken, such as the lease on the El Dorado. Also, Rollins and Dumont provided high-quality work and often would "throw in" extra materials to get this high quality without including these in the price. The consultant had recommended that the firm stop leasing the El Dorado, get another truck, stop taking government jobs, and revise its pricing.

Williams was somewhat daunted by the consultant's report (which the firm had commissioned because of its payment problems), but he arranged for a meeting with John Rollins and Jim Dumont. Although they agreed with the consultant that they needed additional long-term financing, they disagreed with most of the other things in the consultant's report.

"We know what the consultant said, but he doesn't understand the roofing business," said Rollins. "We think that we have a good handle on how to run a business such as ours. Our policy has been simple: we have tried to run a quality operation and use our image and good workmanship to generate a lot of sales volume. That image requires that we put up a good solid front. That's why we rent a nice office and that's why we lease the El Dorado; it gives people a good impression. We don't quibble about a few dollars on the price either or scrimp on the materials. There are others in the business who make more profit per job, but we are trying to develop repeat business. Many of these local governments and agencies have several jobs each year, and we want them to favor us. Most of these jobs are equally profitable with a standard private residential job, although they are slower to pay because of bureaucratic red tape. We believe that our policy is effective; look at our record of sales and earnings growth. However, we need more money to pay bills. We will sell you one third of the stock in the firm for $10,000, which we are going to use to clear up our past-due balances with materials suppliers. If you decide to buy in, we would also appreciate it if you could help us with advice on the financial side of the business. We don't quite understand what happened, and we sure don't want it to happen again."

After this conversation, Williams decided to perform a ratio analysis on the financial statements of Razzle-Dazzle Roofing

Exhibit 2-1. RAZZLE-DAZZLE ROOFING COMPANY

Statement of Income and Retained Earnings (1977–1979)
(Ordered by the Analyst's Method)

Fiscal Year Ending	12/31/77	12/31/78	12/31/79
Sales	$93,125	$127,582	$160,202
Cost of contract materials and cost of outside labor	54,489	85,108	109,848
Gross margin	38,636	42,474	50,354
Other expenses, interest, and officers' salaries	37,200	40,675	47,890
Earnings before taxes	1,436	1,799	2,464
Income taxes (state and federal)	316	396	542
Earnings after taxes	1,120	1,403	1,922
Dividends	0	0	0
Changes in retained earnings	$ 1,120	$ 1,403	$ 1,922

Company (these are presented in Exhibits 2-1 and 2-2). In making his decision as to whether or not to invest in the firm, he knew that profitability and turnover ratios would be most important. He also decided to further analyze the firm by computing debt and liquidity ratios.

Exhibit 2-2 RAZZLE-DAZZLE ROOFING COMPANY

Balance Sheets for Fiscal Years Ending 12/31/77–12/31/79
(Ordered by the Analyst's method)

Fiscal Year Ending	12/31/77	12/31/78	12/31/79
Cash	$ 1,160	$ 770	$ (507)
Accounts receivable	14,327	21,264	28,608
Inventory	3,725	5,103	6,408
Other current assets	202	125	197
Total current assets	19,414	27,262	34,706
Fixed assets (trucks, tools, office supplies, net of depreciation)	4,271	5,679	7,203
Total assets	23,281	29,670	38,143
Wages and accounts payable	6,841	12,794	20,116
Due to bank on truck (current portion)	125	125	375
Contract advances	2,794	3,827	4,806
	9,760	16,746	25,297
Due on truck (LT portion)	6,000	4,000	2,000
Common stock and PIC	4,000	4,000	4,000
Retained earnings	3,521	4,924	6,846
Total equity	7,521	8,924	10,846
Total liabilities and OE	$23,281	$29,670	$38,143

QUESTIONS

1. Compute the total assets turnover and accounts receivable turnover ratios for Razzle-Dazzle for 1977 to 1979. Explain any trends on the basis of information given in the case. If the 1979 industry medians for these ratios are 2.7 and 6.4, respectively, discuss how Razzle-Dazzle had managed these assets relative to the industry for that year.

2. Compute the profitability on sales ratios for Razzle-Dazzle for 1977 to 1979. Explain any trends on the basis of information given. If the 1979 industry median for this ratio is 1.6 per cent, discuss how Razzle-Dazzle's profitability on sales compared to the industry's for that year. Explain any differences on the basis of the facts of the case.

3. In the Dupont system of analysis, return on investment (EAT/Total Assets) is the real measure of management policies and performance. It is the product of the total asset turnover ratio computed in Question 1 and the profitability on sales ratio computed in Question 2. Compute and discuss the ROI of Razzle-Dazzle for 1977–1979; the 1979 industry median is 4.3 per cent. How does this reflect on the firm's policies as stated by Rollins?

4. Compute the current ratio, quick ratio, and total debt to net worth ratios for Razzle-Dazzle for 1977 to 1979. Explain any trends on the basis of information given in the case and previous ratio analysis results. If the 1979 means for these ratios are 1.3, 1.1, and 1.8, respectively, discuss Razzle-Dazzle's liquidity and debt position relative to the industry.

5. Assuming that the $10,000 to be contributed is used as indicated in the case, recompute the 1979 liquidity and debt ratios for Razzle-Dazzle. Compare these to industry standards.

6. What would you advise Williams to do? Why?

7. (At option of the instructor.) Discuss the risk of Razzle-Dazzle as an investment. Is it more or less risky than other small business investments that Williams might consider? The years 1977–79 were those of economic expansion in the United States. Do you think that returns on investment in Razzle-Dazzle would have a high or low beta? Justify your answer.

Magnetics Interplanetary

Ratio Analysis: Credit Decisions

Miss Susan Streusel was a new employee of General Industries Corporation, having recently graduated (in 1980) with a degree in business from a major midwestern university. Her first day on the job had been spent filling out personnel forms, taking a physical examination, and being briefed on personnel policies and the basics of living in Chicago, where General Industries was headquartered. In her second day on the job, she was to start functioning at the position for which she was hired, that of a credit analyst. The day had begun with a discussion of the position with her supervisor, John Szymanski.

"I'm sure you are familiar with the basic analysis methods, Miss Streusel, since you graduated as a finance major," said Szymanski. "However, to clear up any confusion, let me review the methodology; you can get the details when you read our credit policy manual. The basic revenues of our firm, as a manufacturer, come from selling products to other manufacturers, who, in turn, produce consumer goods. Associated with the sale of these products are a number of costs: the costs of materials, direct labor, and so forth. The portion of costs we control here in the credit department is that associated with the credit decision. There are three types of costs in this area: accounts receivable carrying costs, expected bad debt expense, and the cost of collecting accounts receivable. At this point in the development of finance, there are few ways that our firm considers reliable to estimate these costs directly for each firm

13

applying to us for credit. Instead, we try to assess a correlate of these costs—the applicant's credit worthiness—and in this way judge whether the costs of granting credit to the applicant will be greater or less than the revenues the account will produce, net of the other costs of sales. At General Industrial, we assess credit worthiness in a very standard way: we look at five dimensions of the applicant, which are called the 'five Cs of credit.'

"*Capital, collateral,* and *conditions* are the first three of these dimensions, and these attempts to measure the firm's ability to pay off the debt. *Capital* is somewhat of a misnomer and refers to examination of the standard ratio analysis of the credit applicant. I'm sure you are familiar with this. From the standpoint of the credit decision, we believe that liquidity ratios are the most important. This is because our products are sold on 30-day terms and thus represent short-term debt for our customers. Debt ratios, such as the ratio of debt to total assets or debt to net worth, are important also because they are good predictors of our recovery from the debtor if that firm runs into financial problems. Coverage ratios, profitability ratios, and turnover ratios are considered by our firm to be of lesser importance. *Collateral* refers to any unpledged assets that the applicant might offer to pledge in return for credit. *Conditions* mean economic conditions in the industry to which the applicant sells, which are, of course, an important consideration in assessing ability to pay.

"The other two Cs, *character*, and *capacity*, refer to personal factors regarding the applicant's management. *Character* refers to the management's morality—the extent to which it will honestly try to pay back the debt. *Capacity* refers to physical plant and management's talent in making the business work, which can be gauged by its past record in this area.

"One of the products that we sell is technical iron oxide, which is used in making audio tapes. The product we sell is moderately profitable, but selling audio tapes is a tough business because of competition from Japanese producers. We have just received our first order for iron oxide from a fairly large audio tape manufacturer, Magnetics Interplanetary, which has headquarters in Jacksonville, Florida. Here is the credit file on the firm. Evaluate it for a line of credit of about $100,000 and give me your opinion."

Miss Streusel took the credit file to her desk and started to review it. Magnetics had been founded in 1965, and the founder was still operating the firm. In its early years it had acquired several tape manufacturers and tape-manufacturing divisions of

Exhibit 3-1. MAGNETICS INTERPLANETARY

Balance Sheets for Fiscal Years 1975-1979
(Ordered by the Analyst's method; rounded thousands of dollars)

	1975	1976	1977	1978	1979
Cash[1]	$ 159	$ 155	$ 90	$ 80	$ 195
Mar. securities[1]	27	0	0	0	0
Accts. receivable[1]	1,648	1,524	1,838	1,834	1,472
Inventory[1]	2,329	2,436	2,450	2,479	1,969
Other current assets	157	180	178	155	185
Total current assets	4,320	4,295	4,556	4,548	3,821
Fixed assets, net of depreciation[1]	6,613	5,666	5,108	4,187	3,547
Other assets	1,286	1,069	885	782	657
Total assets	12,219	11,030	10,549	9,517	8,025
Due to bank, cur. portion of L.T.D.	39	283	817	300	707
Due to bank, short-term	2,167	1,633	1,634	2,079	933
Accounts payable	2,609	1,805	1,499	1,868	1,139
Accruals	101	131	103	87	91
Total cur. liabilities	4,916	3,852	4,053	4,334	2,870
Due to bank, L.T.D.	5,467	5,183	4,433	4,533	4,887
Common stock[2]	1,887	1,911	1,919	1,919	1,919
Additional P.I.C.	6,364	6,376	6,372	6,373	6,374
Retained earnings	(6,415)	(6,292)	(6,228)	(7,642)	(8,025)
Total O.E.	1,836	1,995	2,063	650	268
Total Lia. and O.E.	$12,219	$11,030	$10,549	$ 9,517	$ 8,025

[1] These assets are pledged as collateral for loans from banks.
[2] As of 12/31/79, 1,919,000 shares were outstanding. Common stock traded at an average price of $0.75 per share during fiscal 1979.

Exhibit 3-2. MAGNETICS INTERPLANETARY

Statement of Income and Retained Earnings for Fiscal Year 1975–1979
(Ordered by the Analyst's method; rounded thousands of dollars)

	1975	1976	1977	1978	1979
Net sales	$ 8,311	$ 9,329	$10,156	$10,987	$ 9,571
Cost of goods sold	7,777	6,610	7,007	8,357	7,163
Gross margin on sales	534	2,719	3,149	2,630	2,408
Selling, Admin., and General Expenses	7,119	2,531	3,064	4,044	2,791
Earnings before taxes	(6,585)	188	85	(1,414)	(383)
Taxes	0	65	21	0	0
Earnings after taxes	(6,585)	123	64	(1,414)	(383)
Beginning ret. earn.	170	(6,415)	(6,292)	(6,228)	(7,642)
Ending ret. earnings	$(6,415)	$(6,292)	$ (6,228)	$ (7,642)	$(8,025)

other firms. These acquisitions were made for stock and cash (the firm's stock was traded over-the-counter). The firm's sales had grown rapidly initially, but had been stagnant over the last five years (Magnetics' balance sheets and income statements for the fiscal years 1975-1979 are presented in Exhibits 3-1 and 3-2.) During the last five years, the firm had recorded three years of after-tax losses and two years of profits. Magnetics' management gave numerous reasons for this unstable pattern of profitability: high interest rates, unexpectedly high raw material and labor costs, Japanese competition, and trucking industry strikes.

The firm's long-term debt was owed to bank lenders. The bank lending agreement included covenants that had at times been violated, but Magnetics had always been able to obtain waivers from bank lenders so the firm was not considered in default. Also, Magnetics had renegotiated the terms of payment on this debt in 1979, rearranging and lengthening the repayment schedule. Because of these problems and the firm's record in the profits area, the firm's independent auditor had issued a qualified opinion regarding the firm's 1979 financial statements. The firm in the past capitalized certain research expenses, but

Exhibit 3-3. MAGNETICS INTERPLANETARY

Partial Survey of Trade Suppliers

Supplier Code	Highest Amount Owed	Currently Owed	Currently Past Due	Terms of Sale	Payments
5	$ 1,500	$ 0	$ 0	Now COD	--------------------
7	150	0	0	Now COD	--------------------
11	9,000	0	0	Now COD	--------------------
27	19,000	8,400	0	N 10 prox.	ppt.-slow 30 days
38	2,900	0	0	Now COD	--------------------
87	67,000	67,000	67,000	N 30 days	ppt.-slow 60 days
111	12,900	4,000	0	N 30 days	ppt.-slow 30 days
112	2,000	700	0	N 30 days	slow 45– 60 days
236	180	0	0	Check in advance	--------------------
275	500	0	0	N 30 days	placed for collection
311	$19,540	$15,930	$11,000	N 30 days	slow 45 days

these accounting procedures had been revised (the statements in Exhibits 3-1 and 3-2 reflect this revision.)

Magnetics' relationship with creditors had at times been strained. The firm had continuously been sued by suppliers for past-due trade balances, and commonly had as many as forty unsettled judgments, some for very small amounts (less than $1,000), but these suits were eventually settled. The credit file for Magnetics also contained a current trade clearance, which listed the firm's payments to several suppliers (see Exhibit 3-3). When asked about the condition of payments to suppliers by trade reporting agencies, Magnetics' management attributed any problems to slow collection of their own receivables.

QUESTIONS

1. Compute Magnetics' current and quick ratios for the fiscal years 1975-1979. If the 1979 industry median for these ratios are 1.70 and 0.80, how does the firm compare with other industry credit applicants from this industry in terms of liquidity? Are there any trends in these ratios?

2. Compute Magnetics' debt ratios (total debt to total assets and total debt to net worth) for the fiscal years 1975-1979. If the 1979 industry medians for these ratios are 0.60 and 1.50, how does the firm compare with other industry credit applicants in terms of the safety of debt? Are there any trends in these ratios?

3. Based on your answers to Questions 1 and 2, assess Magnetics on the dimension of credit worthiness called capital relative to the industry.

4. Is there any collateral available to General Industries to use to secure the transaction?

5. Give an assessment of the economic conditions in Magnetics' industry.

6. Compute the average collection period for Magnetics for 1979. If Magnetics' terms of sale to its customers are 45 days, is the firm's contention that its receivables are significantly slow borne out by this statistic? Why or why not?

7. Based on your answer to Question 6 and the data in the case, assess Magnetics management's character and capacity.

8. What should Susan Streusel recommend to Szymanski regarding a line of credit for Magnetics?

9. (At option of the instructor.) In a partial attempt to remove the ambiguity in standard credit analysis, efforts have been made to forecast default statistically. Perhaps the most

noted research has been by Edward I. Altman.* He produced the following forecasting equation:

$$Z = .012\left(\frac{WC}{TA}\right) + .014\left(\frac{RE}{TA}\right) + .033\left(\frac{EBIT}{TA}\right)$$
$$+ .006\left(\frac{equity}{debt}\right) + .999\left(\frac{S}{TA}\right)$$

where: Z = score on the function

WC/TA = ratio of working capital to total assets (expressed as a per cent)

RE/TA = ratio of retained earnings to total assets (expressed as a per cent)

$EBIT/TA$ = ratio of earnings before interest and taxes to total assets (expressed as a per cent)

equity/debt = ratio of market value of equity to book value of total debt (expressed as a per cent)

S/TA = ratio of sales to total assets (expressed as a ratio)

For his sample, he found that firms with scores less than 1.81 always failed within one year and firms with scores greater than 2.99 never failed within one year. The score range of 1.81 to 2.99 contained some failing and some nonfailing firms. Compute Magnetics' Z score for 1979. You may assume that interest expense for that year was $525,000. Does this change your answer to Question 8?

*See his "Financial Ratios, Discriminant Analysis, and the Prediction of Corporate Bankruptcy," *Journal of Finance*, September 1968.

Corbin's Cabinet Doors

Breakeven Analysis

When John Corbin had received his master's degree in engineering from an eastern university, he had taken a job as a process engineer with a large corporation. In late 1969, he had an idea for a new way to make cabinet doors for kitchen cabinets. At the time, there were three types of such doors available: metal, wooden, and composition, each produced in different ways. The metal doors were stamped out of sheetmetal and then painted. The wooden doors were cut from raw pieces of wooden plank, carved, and finished. The composition doors were produced by a pressing process. John Corbin, however, had worked on a method of forming cabinet doors out of other materials. In his process, a metal mold was first constructed including whatever features were desired for the cabinet face: moldings, designs, and so on. Plastic materials were added to the mold and allowed to set. With proper coloring of the plastic and careful mold design, the doors were similar in appearance to wooden ones. During 1970, 1971, and early 1972, he thought he had the technical aspects sufficiently developed that the doors could be produced on a commercial basis. In July 1972, he quit his job and formed Corbin's Cabinet Doors, in his hometown of Ashtabula, Ohio. The remainder of 1972 was spent setting up the plant and making various trial runs and adjustments. There were some initial difficulties in producing consistently high-quality output, but these were eventually solved.

The fiscal year ending on December 31, 1973 was the first full year of the firm's operations. Much to Corbin's surprise, the firm took a small loss. (The firm's financial statements are presented in Exhibit 4-1 and 4-2). Even though the cabinet doors produced were of good quality and priced cheaper than comparable wooden doors, the firm's sales had been much below production capacity. Because the process was highly technical, Corbin had concentrated on the production end of the business in 1973; sales were made on a commission basis by a sales agency that also handled other home remodeling and construction products. Upon making inquiries among several of the salesmen involved, Corbin found that there had been some initial resistance to the door because of unfamiliarity with the materials involved. The product was perceived as artificial in the sense that it was not made from natural materials, and thus would not be as readily acceptable to consumers. Further, there was some concern that the screws used to secure the hinges to cabinet doors would either not hold in the material used in Corbin's doors or would be difficult to attach. However, builders and modelers were gradually becoming familiar with the product, and the salesmen expected that sales would rise during the coming year.

This prospect heartened Corbin considerably; he wondered, however, how changes in sales would affect his firm's profit-

Exhibit 4-1. CORBIN'S CABINET DOORS

Balance Sheet as of December 31, 1973

Cash on deposit	$ 1,830.85
Accounts receivable	14,612.24
Inventory	17,496.00
Total current assets	33,939.09
Gross fixed assets	38,582.15
Reserve for depreciation	12,594.00
Net fixed assets	29,988.15
Total assets	$59,927.24
Accounts payable	12,136.85
Accrued expenses	3,673.54
Total current liabilities	15,810.39
Common stock (owned by John Corbin)	46,000.00
Retained earnings	(1,883.15)
Total stockholders' equity	44,116.85
Total liabilities and owners' equity	$59,927.24

Exhibit 4-2. CORBIN'S CABINET DOORS

Statement of Income for Fiscal 1973

Sales (83,000 units sold)	$182,600.00
Raw materials purchases	80,659.20
Manufacturing payroll	32,874.49
Insurance	13,061.36
Rent	3,409.92
Office expenses	4,534.69
Manufacturing overhead	5,545.78
Administrative and engineering payroll	28,278.70
Sales commission	1,826.00
Depreciation	12,594.00
Miscellaneous other expenses	1,699.01
Net income	$ (1,883.15)

ability. He knew that the "Raw Materials Purchases" entry on his firm's Statement of Income represented mostly the plastic materials used in the manufacturing process; the metal molds had been fabricated in 1971 and 1972, and Corbin wanted to use these designs for several more years. "Manufacturing Payroll" included all payments to the in-plant workers, including social security and workman's compensation; the "Insurance" entry referred to fire, property, and casualty insurance. "Rent" on the office and plant was fixed by the lease for the next three years. "Manufacturing Overhead" was the electricity, repair work, and so on necessary to keep the firm's machinery running. "Depreciation" was on a straight line basis. "Office Expenses," "Administrative and Engineering Payroll," and "Other Expenses" related to salaries paid to office personnel (the firm's secretary and part-time accountant).

QUESTIONS

1. Generate a breakeven chart (graph) relating income, costs, and units produced and sold. Justify any assumptions regarding which costs are fixed and which are variable. Indicate on the chart the breakeven points based on earnings and cash flow. You may assume that all variable costs vary linearly with sales based on fiscal 1973's proportion.

2. Calculate the earnings and cash breakeven points.

3. Compute the degree of operating leverage at the 1973 sales volume and at a sales volume of 100,000 units. What are the significance of these figures? How much profit will the firm make

if production and sales are 100,000 units (obtain results graphically and by generating a pro forma income statement)?

4. Given that sales for his firm are likely to increase in the future, should Corbin be optimistic or pessimistic about the firm's future? Why or why not?

5. (At option of instructor.) Assume that a large builder, such as Ryan Homes, decided to place a large order with Corbin. Would it be correct to extrapolate the breakeven chart and read profit figures for much, much larger sales volumes? Why or why not?

6. (At option of the instructor.) Suppose Corbin had the opportunity to obtain additional machinery that would result in yearly total fixed costs of $75,000, including depreciation of $20,000, and variable costs of $1.25 per unit. Discuss the effects of this change relative to the current costs structure; contrast profit results and breakeven points with those achieved under the current system.

Original Chemical Company (A)

Financial Forecasting and Proforma Statements

Original Chemical Company was a publicly owned firm with common shares traded on the New York Stock Exchange. The firm had been started in the 1920s and had grown internally until the mid-1960s. Between 1966 and 1975, the firm acquired several smaller chemical companies, usually by an exchange of common stock, although a cash exchange was sometimes involved. Fourteen firms, domestic and foreign, were acquired during this period. These acquisitions enabled Original Chemical to broaden considerably its line of chemicals into several business areas in which the firm had no previous dealings: detergents, certain plastics, and petrochemical products. In 1976, however, the firm withdrew from the retailing end of the petrochemical business by selling its forty gasoline service stations and decided to concentrate on the production and sale of industrial chemical products.

As of late 1979, the firm produced and sold a broad line of chemicals for industrial use, including specialty chemicals, commercial petroleum products, and plastics. Because of its long experience in the chemicals industry and considerable technical expertise, the firm did substantial business in products formulated to meet customer specifications. The firm maintained fifteen domestic manufacturing locations and a similar number of research and applications laboratories. The majority of the firm's six foreign subsidiaries were consolidated on the firm's balance sheet, which is presented as Exhibit 5-1.

Exhibit 5-1. ORIGINAL CHEMICAL COMPANY (A)

Consolidated Balance Sheets as of December 31
(Rounded thousands of dollars; ordered by the
Accountant's method)

	1979 (preliminary)	1978	1977
Cash and marketable securities	$ 27,107	$ 18,761	$ 11,600
Accounts receivable	67,951	60,349	52,631
Inventories	56,946	49,804	44,592
Prepaid expenses and other CA	2,730	2,645	3,496
Total CA	154,734	131,559	112,319
Gross property, plant, and equipment	220,050	212,830	198,230
Accumulated depreciation	111,906	103,172	94,977
Net property, plant, and equipment	108,144	109,658	103,253
Investment in nonconsolidated affiliates	5,215	4,988	6,941
Excess of acquisition cost over book value of acquired firms	10,030	10,090	10,244
Other assets	4,430	6,877	7,902
Total assets	282,553	263,173	240,659
Notes payable to bank	4,070	2,687	3,378
Accts. payable to trade creditors	52,927	48,583	41,625
Dividends payable	1,795	1,640	1,409
Income taxes payable	3,054	3,143	220
Total current liabilities	61,846	56,053	46,632
Long-term debt	55,448	57,770	59,420
Deferred credits	21,323	19,110	16,652
Common stock ($5 par)	22,878	22,477	21,939
Capital surplus	3,355	2,679	2,884
Retained earnings	117,703	105,084	93,132
Total stockholders' equity	143,936	130,240	117,955
Total liabilities and owners' equity	$282,553	$263,173	$240,659

The firm's long-term debt consisted of a number of issues, some with sinking funds and some without. Three of these issues had principal payments due in 1980: (1) $300,000 was due on a 5 per cent bond issue that had been outstanding since 1962; (2) $750,000 was due on an issue of convertible subordinated debentures issued in 1970; and (3) $1,000,000 was due on a term loan from an insurance company. These principal amounts are not included in current liabilities in the preliminary balance sheet for December 31, 1979.

It was Original Chemical's policy to issue new financing instruments only every three or four years, rather than each year, to finance the firm's expansion. In this way, the firm could sell larger issues and thus, it was thought, reduce overall flotation costs. In the interim between these security issues, the firm financed the necessary deficits by borrowing from a bank on a note basis.

In early 1980 Joan Laio was employed as one of Original Chemical's financial analysts. Early in each year she was charged with preparing a proforma balance sheet and income statement for the firm, forecasting the firm's expected financial position at the end of the upcoming fiscal year assuming no new long-term financing through a security issue. This statement was used by the firm's financial vice-president to advise the bank of the amount the firm expected to borrow during the upcoming year.

Exhibit 5-2. ORIGINAL CHEMICAL COMPANY (A)

Consolidated Statements of Income and Retained Earnings
for Fiscal Years Ending December 31
(Rounded thousands of dollars;
ordered by Accountant's method)

	1979 (preliminary)	1978	1977
Net sales	$505,930	$452,766	$422,187
Cost of sales	410,917	365,476	347,702
Selling and administrative expenses	44,277	39,182	35,050
Depreciation, depletion, and amortization	13,863	12,121	11,093
Interest expense	4,330	4,321	4,918
Operating income	32,543	31,666	23,424
Other income	2,314	1,968	3,722
Other expenses	0	0	0
Earnings before taxes	34,857	33,634	23,706
Income taxes	15,142	15,154	11,093
Earnings after taxes	19,715	18,480	12,613
Dividends on common stock	7,096	6,528	5,640
Contributions to retained earnings	$ 12,619	$ 11,952	$ 6,973

In forecasting the firm's expected financial position as of December 31, 1980, Ms. Laio first sought advice from the marketing research department. She was told that the most likely sales level would result in a 7.66 per cent increase in dollar sales volume from the level achieved in fiscal 1979. This estimate was based on a linear regression forecast. The firm's capital budget and noncash expense schedules for 1980 had already been determined: a total of $19.8 million in new property, plant, and equipment was to be purchased; depreciation for the year would total $9.2 million; and other noncash expenses, $5.7 million. On the basis of preliminary estimates, she expected interest expense to total $5.3 million and other income to be approximately $2 million. Beyond this, she wanted to forecast other financial statement entries on either a per cent of sales or a spot basis—per cent of sales if the entry seemed likely to increase directly with sales based on financial theory or the firm's experience, or spot basis (direct estimate of the dollar amount involved) if the entry was not linked to sales. Prior years' income statements are presented in Exhibit 5–2; correlations between several financial statement entries and sales are presented in Exhibit 5–3.

Exhibit 5–3. ORIGINAL CHEMICAL COMPANY (A)

Pearson Product-Moment Correlation Coefficients Between Sales and Other Financial Statement Entries (Based on 17 data points 1962–1979)

Statement entry	Correlation with fiscal sales
Cost of sales	.99958
Selling and administrative expenses	.98464
Accounts receivable	.98761
Inventories	.98724
Accounts payable	.73821

QUESTIONS

1. On the basis of financial theory, empirical relationships, and the facts of the case, indicate the most appropriate way for Ms. Laio to forecast the following entries over the upcoming one-year period. Justify your choice of the per cent-of-sales or

spot method in each of the following:
    Cost of sales
    Selling and administrative expenses
    Dividends on common stock
    Dividends payable
    Cash and marketable securities
    Accounts receivable
    Inventories
    Prepaid expenses and other current assets
    Investment in nonconsolidated affiliates
    Excess of acquisition cost over book value of affiliated firms
    Other assets
    Accounts payable to trade creditors
    Deferred credits

2. Generate a proforma statement of income and changes in retained earnings for Original Chemical for fiscal 1980.

3. Generate a proforma balance sheet for Original Chemical as of December 31, 1980; short-term notes due to the bank will be the balancing item. On the basis of these figures, how much should the financial vice-president arrange to borrow?

4. (At option of the instructor.) What does Exhibit 5–3 indicate regarding the relationships between the variables listed and sales for Original Chemical? Why? How does this help you in answering Question 1?

Deutschland Chemicals U.S.

Cash Budgeting

Deutschland Chemical U.S. was a subsidiary of a large German chemical firm. The parent company was technologically progressive and had developed a number of technologies (new products and production processes) that it believed would give it an advantage in the U.S. market. In the late 1950s the parent company had started a joint venture (with an American firm) in the United States to exploit these technologies. In the mid-1960s, because of antitrust problems, the American partner had sold its interest in the joint venture to the German firm. The German owners then changed the firm's name to Deutschland Chemical U.S.

In late 1978, Deutschland Chemical U.S. was broken into two divisions on the basis of product lines: the Chemicals Division and the Plastics Division. The plants for these divisions were located in several states close to suppliers of raw materials. The Chemicals Division produced a group of complex industrial chemicals that were sold to other firms, who then turned these chemicals into consumer goods. Because the processes necessary to turn these chemicals into consumer goods were quite capital-intensive, customers of the Chemical Division tended to be large, stable, and well-financed firms. This characteristic, combined with the generous discount offered on products of this division for prompt payment (terms of sale were 2 per cent thirty days, net thirty-one days) meant that most of this division's customers paid quite promptly. The firm usually estimated that 80 per cent of all the sales of this division would be collected one month following the sale, the remainder being collected two months following the sale. The products of the Chemicals Division were quite profitable, with purchases of direct materials accounting for only 40 per cent of sales volume. These purchases were made in the month of the sale and paid for in the following month (estimates of sales for both divisions of Deutschland Chemical U.S. for each month of 1979 are provided in Exhibit 6-1).

Unlike the Chemical Division, the Plastics Division sold to small, marginally profitable firms and did not offer cash discounts (terms of sale were net thirty days). The firm usually estimated that only 40 per cent of the sales of this division would be collected one month following the sale, with 50 per cent collected the second month following the sale, and the remaining 10 per cent, the third month following the sale. As with the Chemicals Division, purchases of direct materials for the Plactics Division were made in the month of the sale and paid for in the following month. However, the products sold by the Plastics Division were not as profitable and these purchases amounted to 60 per cent of sales for this division. Also, as with

Exhibit 6-1. DEUTSCHLAND CHEMICALS U.S.

Forecast of Gross Sales (Net of Returns and Allowances but Unadjusted for Payment Discounts) by Month for 1979; Actual Figures Shown for Late 1978

Month	Chemical Division Gross Sales	Plastics Division Gross Sales
September 1978	$ 7,000,000 (actual)	$5,500,000 (actual)
October 1978	7,000,000 "	3,500,000 "
November 1978	7,500,000 "	2,000,000 "
December 1978	8,000,000 "	2,000,000 "
January 1979	10,000,000 (estimated)	2,000,000 (estimated)
February 1979	12,000,000 "	3,000,000 "
March 1979	14,000,000 "	4,000,000 "
April 1979	16,000,000 "	5,000,000 "
May 1979	10,000,000 "	6,000,000 "
June 1979	9,000,000 "	7,000,000 "
July 1979	8,000,000 "	8,000,000 "
August 1979	8,000,000 "	7,000,000 "
September 1979	7,500,000 "	6,000,000 "
October 1979	7,500,000 "	4,000,000 "
November 1979	8,000,000 "	2,000,000 "
December 1979	$ 8,500,000 "	$2,000,000 "

Exhibit 6-2. DEUTSCHLAND CHEMICALS U.S.

Schedule of Notes Due to Bank for 1979

Month		Note Payments Due
January	1979	$1,000,000
February	1979	2,000,000
March	1979	0
April	1979	0
May	1979	0
June	1979	0
July	1979	0
August	1979	1,000,000
September	1979	0
October	1979	0
November	1979	1,000,000
December	1979	$2,000,000

sales of the Chemical Division, sales of the Plastics Division were somewhat seasonal.

For 1979, the firm had estimated that it would pay $5 million per month in rents, selling and administrative expenses, and salaries of production employees. The firm had also estimated taxes, due in March, June, September, and December at $4.2 million per payment. The firm also had bank notes due at various times during the year (a schedule of these is provided in Exhibit 6-2). Also, the firm planned to spend $8 million in capital expenditures for the acquisition of land and buildings. This money was to be spent in December 1979.

QUESTIONS

1. Generate a schedule of cash receipts for the firm on a monthly basis for 1979. (Keep in mind that a 2 per cent discount applies to all collections made in the first month on sales by the Chemicals Division). You may assume throughout the questions that income from the investment of surplus cash and interest on bank loans necessary to maintain the desired level of cash are negligible.

2. Generate a schedule of cash disbursements for the firm on a monthly basis for 1979.

3. Generate a monthly cash forecast for the firm for 1979. You may assume that the desired level of cash is $3 million, that this is the firm's cash balance as of December 31, 1978, and that this desired level of cash will not change during 1979.

4. During what months will there be net cash inflows? Outflows? What causes this?

5. (At option of the instructor.) Generate a table of cumulative necessary borrowings on surplus cash balances for the firm. On the basis of current yields or government securities and your knowledge of the yield curve, how should surplus cash be invested? How much will be earned on these investments?

Basic Industries, Inc.

Sources and Applications of Funds

Basic Industries, Inc. was a large firm with headquarters in the Midwest. The firm was involved in various lines of business through its several divisions. Among these enterprises was the development and construction of steelmaking facilities in the United States and abroad. From the 1950s into the 1970s the firm had constructed or played a major part in designing steel mills in Chile, the Philippines, Venezuela, Egypt, and Turkey. Projects of this sort, as well as several of the firm's other business lines, required extensive capital and other expenditures. In late 1979 the firm was trying to project its funds needs for the upcoming year and to trace the flows of funds through the firm.

In 1978 the firm had increased its debt to finance investments and to expand working capital, manufacturing, and other operations. During that year, as interim financing, the firm had issued commercial paper. This had been liquidated by December 31, 1978 and replaced by three other financing instruments: (1) a long-term promissory note to an insurance company; (2) an issue of industrial revenue bonds (additional bonds of this sort were also issued in early 1979); and (3) an expanded revolving bank credit agreement. Part of the amount due on the previous bank credit line was carried over into the new arrangement, and the balance of $18,750,000 was converted into a note payable in the first quarter of 1980.

During 1979 the firm had continued to increase its debt to finance small acquisitions and to meet working capital requirements. In October 1979, Carol Furbee, a junior financial analyst with the firm, was given the assignment of generating the firm's by-quarter sources and applications of funds statements as projected for 1980. To do this, she first obtained a projected income statement for Basic Industries for fiscal 1980 (see Exhibit 7-1). On the basis of prior years' quarterly results, she then developed a table spreading several of these items over the quarters of the firm's fiscal year (see Exhibit 7-2).

This done, she turned to balance sheet items. It was the firm's standard procedure to make quarterly funds flow projections on a consolidated working capital basis, that is, with all the working capital accounts (current assets and liabilities) aggregated. As part of another project, Ms. Furbee had already projected the firm's required levels of working capital to support sales volumes, exclusive of any borrowings or other transactions on note and other financing instrument accounts, to be $215,920,000 as of December 31, 1979; $215,082,000 at the end of the first quarter of 1980; $215,895,000 at the end of the second quarter; $244,902,000 at the end of the third quarter; and $217,604,000 by the end of the fourth quarter. Deferred taxes and other deferred expenses were expected to increase by $2,521,000 between December 31, 1979 and March 31, 1980; increase by another $3,841,000 between March 31, 1980 and June 30, 1980; increase again by another $1,688,000 between June 30, 1980 and September 30, 1980; and finally fall by $196,000 between September 30, 1980 and year-end. Payments on the firm's long-term debt would reduce this debt by $2,011,000 per quarter. Capital expenditures for the year,

Exhibit 7-1. BASIC INDUSTRIES, INC.

Abbreviated Projected Statement of Income and Retained Earnings for Fiscal 1980 (rounded thousands of dollars)

Sales	$1,539,818
Expenses and interest	1,340,087
Earnings before depreciation, depletion, and taxes	199,731
Depreciation and depletion	63,018
Earnings before taxes	136,713
Taxes	65,622
Net income	71,091
Equity earnings (losses) from unconsolidated subsidiaries	(931)
Common dividends	25,115
Additions to retained earnings	$ 45,045

Exhibit 7-2. BASIC INDUSTRIES, INC.

Projected Portions of Yearly Income Statement Items
to Occur in Fiscal 1980, by Quarter

	Quarter ending			
Item	3/31/80	6/30/80	9/30/80	12/31/80
Sales	0.180	0.254	0.283	0.283
Net income	0.041	0.278	0.333	0.348
Depreciation and depletion	0.188	0.251	0.280	0.281
Dividends	0.250	0.250	0.250	0.250
Equity earnings or losses from uncon- solidated subsidiaries	0.250	0.250	0.250	0.250

Ms. Furbee found, were to total $164,578,000; this figure was
obtained from progress reports on construction in progress and
records of previously approved projects to be started in 1980.
Of this, 23.2 per cent was to be spent in the first quarter, 16.3
per cent in the second quarter, 26.5 per cent in the third
quarter, and the remaining 34.0 per cent in the fourth quarter.
All other cash flows, including contributions to the employees'
savings plan, small amounts of common stock to be sold, and
similar miscellaneous items, were expected to total $1,636,000
in funds inflows during each quarter.

QUESTIONS

1. Generate sources and applications of funds statements for
each quarter of 1980 on the basis of projections given in the
case. The necessary borrowings on the rotating credit line will
be the balancing item. Be sure to include a column expressing
for each quarter each source or application of funds as a per
cent of total funds flow.

2. The firm's new rotating credit line has a maximum borrowing limit of $90 million. If the beginning (December 31, 1979)
balance on this line is $15 million, do the firm's plans require
that the borrowing limit be exceeded at any quarter-end during
1980? Explain your answer.

3. On the basis of your answer to Question 1, what are to be
the major funds flows for Basic Industries during 1980? What
does this say about the plans of the firm?

4. (At option of the instructor.) In capital budgeting analysis, it is often said that net cash flow for a project during its operating periods equals earnings after taxes plus depreciation (assuming, of course, that all capital expenses occur at time zero). Contrast this with the cash flows calculated in a flow-of-funds statement such as that generated in response to Question 1. Include in your answer the assumptions necessary for the two methods to produce equivalent cash flow estimates.

PART II

Current Asset Management

Monsanto Co.*

Management of Cash and Marketable Securities

Besides cooking up hundreds of plastics, weed killers, and various chemicals, Monsanto Co. constantly stirs a huge pot of cash.

The man in the financial kitchen of the big chemical company, which rang up $5 billion in sales last year, is Robert A. Westoby. As U.S. cash manager, Mr. Westoby—day in and day out—moves around millions of dollars with the quick finesse of a short order cook.

His days at Monsanto's sprawling suburban headquarters here begin early. At 8 A.M. a computer terminal in a carpeted corridor outside his small corner office signals the start. It jumps to life with a staccato chatter and swiftly prints out the overnight figures of Monsanto's checking account balances at a large New York bank. The machine's message: Today, Mr. Westoby is sitting atop a small mountain of cash.

It is important to Monsanto that Mr. Westoby move that mountain in a hurry. High money market interest rates, currently in excess of 10%, offer opportunities for quick earnings; a million dollars, rather than sitting idle in a corporate checking account, can earn more than $100,000 a year at little risk.

*The body of this case is an article that originally appeared in *The Wall Street Journal*, Aug. 13, 1979, pp. 1 and 18, under the title "Corporate Investor: Managing the Money for Big Firms Requires Many Quick Decisions" by Daniel Hertzberg. Reprinted by permission of *The Wall Street Journal*, © Dow Jones and Company, Inc., 1979. All rights reserved.

"Time spent in cash management is well spent," says Frank Kneisel, treasurer of Champion International Corp.

Lately, more and more U.S. companies have been improving their cash management. Aided by computerization, they can balance their checking accounts quickly each day and no longer need to keep a cushion of extra cash on deposit. Meanwhile, the big banks are eagerly competing for their business. And perhaps as a result of the stepped-up pace of the action, a new, more aggressive breed of corporate cash manager has arrived on the scene, experts say.

"I can remember five years ago about half the asset managers you'd call were about to retire," says Timothy W. Thompson, vice-president and head of world-wide financial services for New York's Chemical Bank. "Now 80% are sharp young MBAs."

But, other observers say, not all companies are pushing cash management. "You would be shocked how thin some major companies are in that department," a banker comments.

VALUE OF THE PORTFOLIO

At Monsanto, Mr. Westoby tracks the tens of millions of dollars flowing daily through the company's bank accounts around the nation. Every idle dollar that he can squeeze out of Monsanto's balances goes quickly into high-yielding money-market investments, such as Treasury Bills, federal agency securities, certificates of deposit sold by major U.S. banks, bankers acceptances, bank guaranteed trade bills, and top-grade commercial paper (corporate IOUs).

All told, he runs a short-term investment portfolio that ranges, depending on the time of year, from $150 million to $350 million. And quite unlike a genteel coupon-clipping operation, the portfolio is *managed*.

A 40-year-old Canadian with horn-rimmed glasses, Mr. Westoby takes off his jacket, leans back in his swivel chair, and lights up a cigarette. His first job is to find out how much idle cash he has on hand for the day. In addition to the data from the computer terminal, his staff of five women is at work telephoning Monsanto's other banks to assemble the latest information on checking account balances.

Meanwhile, his own phone starts ringing, and it won't stop all morning. On a busy day, his secretary logs up to 90 incoming calls, mainly bankers soliciting deposits and dealers offering to sell money market investments to Monsanto. The dealers, particularly, also perform a significant service. They supply valuable information on rapidly changing conditions in the money markets.

"Hi, Ned," Mr. Westoby greets a money-market trader at a New York bank. "We'll have our cash figures in a few minutes," he tells another dealer. "What you got that's good and short?" he asks a third.

CLOSE TIES IMPORTANT

Later, Mr. Westoby explains, "This job goes south in a hurry if you can't maintain good relationships with bankers and dealers." He says he deals on a "very, very, regular basis" with traders at half-a-dozen big banks and securities firms in New York, Chicago, and San Francisco. Stressing the dealers' importance as a "source of up-to-date information on the market," he adds, "If you don't have good contacts, you can get shafted."

Neatly placed on top of Mr. Westoby's desk are the tools of his trade: two telephones, a pad of "trade tickets" to record transactions, and a small calculator plugged into a wall socket. With these tools, he works with his raw material: Monsanto's pile of investable cash, which, a company official says, has multiplied at least threefold since the early 1970s.

Monsanto isn't unusual; many companies are flush with cash. At the end of the first quarter of 1979, U.S. nonfinancial corporations held cash and marketable securities totaling $138.1 billion, up from $116.6 billion in 1975. John W. Field, Jr., a vice-president at Morgan Guaranty Trust Co. in New York, says the 1974 credit crunch, during which some corporations got caught short of cash, led to a general retrenchment and "a tremendous buildup in short-term investment portfolios." Although these portfolios have declined a bit, he says, "there's still one hell of a lot of cash around."

Another sign that "companies are awash in liquidity," as one banker puts it, is the record $100 billion market in commercial paper, which enables major companies to bypass banks and lend directly to one another. However, economists caution that many cash-rich corporations also have run up huge amounts of short-term debt.

It's 9:50 A.M. Sandy Kennedy, one of Mr. Westoby's assistants, walks into his office. "I'd like for you to invest 30," she says—verbal shorthand for the $30 million available that day in idle cash and maturing investments. But he already has swung into action.

Moments earlier, with the words, "Okay, let's pick up five

overnight," Mr. Westoby had agreed to buy $5 million in government securities from a dealer who will buy them back the next day at a slightly higher price. Known as a repurchase agreement, or "repo" in market slang, the transaction is equivalent to a one-day loan to the dealer with government securities serving as collateral.

SEASONAL CASH FLOWS

"Okay, Let's do some work," Mr. Westoby exclaims. His pace on the telephone quickens. He tells a Chicago dealer, "I got five loose cash hanging around." He listens to an offer but shakes his head, "No, no."

A dealer in Treasury bills gets on the line.

"Let's do 10," Mr. Westoby suggests. "You got numbers?" He swiftly punches his calculator to work out the yields.

"That's 10 more out of the way," Mr. Westoby declares. He has just bought $10 million in Treasury bills maturing in just three days.

Monsanto's cash, like that of many companies, flows in seasonal patterns. In the Spring, the inflow is heavy, swollen by advance payments for agricultural chemicals. As the year progresses, the level of cash subsides. The cash manager must periodically set aside big sums to meet payrolls, dividends on stock, and tax bills.

The rate of these cash flows can be influenced by cash managers. A simple but effective device is the "lockbox," a post-office box used as a bill-collection system and monitored by a bank. Bypassing corporate headquarters in this way speeds bill collections. Monsanto, for example, has 22 lockboxes scattered around the U.S.

On the other side of the ledger, some cash managers try to slow the outflow of corporate money. Some, for example, delay payments on bills by paying East Coast bills with checks drawn on a West Coast bank. (Mr. Westoby says Monsanto doesn't do this, however.)

Other cash managers try—sometimes successfully—to get banks to cut the standard 10% compensatory balances, the sums that companies must keep on deposit in checking accounts to compensate for unused bank credit lines. "Banks don't go out of their way to educate you if you have too much money in the accounts," Champion International's Mr. Kneisel says.

However, many banks are eager to help their corporate customers. Because of their adoption of computer technology, corporate cash managers no longer have to spend most of each morning telephoning to find out what their cash balances are; rather, through equipment like the computer terminal near Mr. Westoby's office, major banks report electronically to corporate customers the cash balances in bank accounts around the world. In addition, the banks offer rapid electronic transfers of funds. And they are competing to market slick, new computer-based cash-management systems, such as Chase Manhattan Bank's Infocash, Chemical's ChemLink and Morgan's MARS.

"It's gotten to the point that if you don't come up with a new bell or whistle once a month, you've lost your competitiveness," a West Coast banker wryly complains. Bankers say such non-credit services can lead to a role in supplying credit to a major corporation.

EASING GUIDELINES

In their own search for higher yields, some corporations have loosened once-restrictive investment guidelines. But conservatism remains the rule. U.S. corporate cash is overwhelmingly invested in the domestic money market, where risk is deemed less than overseas and assets can be converted into cash quickly. "We're most concerned with safety and liquidity," says Stephen Nightingdale, treasurer of Union Carbide Corp., in a typical comment.

Monsanto lets Mr. Westoby buy Eurodollar certificates of deposit (CDs sold by overseas branches of U.S. banks), but he rules out money market instruments denominated in foreign currencies, Treasury bill futures, and corporate stocks. To minimize foreign-currency losses, the company says it has begun "major" financial hedging through purchases of forward currency contracts in the British pound, the Belgian franc, and other currencies in which it has significant exposure. Mr. Westoby says he doesn't manage overseas accounts, however; those moneys are handled abroad.

According to Mr. Westoby, the Monsanto portfolio in the U.S. currently yields an average 10.65% on maturities averaging between 60 and 270 days. He also estimates that the active portfolio trading in which he engages is probably worth one quarter of a percentage point in additional yield. On a $300 million portfolio, for example, that amounts to $750,000 a year.

ANOTHER QUICK DEAL

Then Mr. Westoby quickly seals a deal to buy $5 million in Federal Farm Credit System notes that mature in about two months and yield about 10%.

Now, Mr. Westoby is talking with two dealers at once, cradling a phone in each hand. Jokingly, he picks up a call moments later with the words, "God speaks."

At 10:15 A.M. he completes a $10 million repurchase agreement. He leans back in his chair and exclaims, "That's the $30 million done."

During much of the rest of the day, Mr. Westoby meets separately with representatives of two banks involved in Monsanto's credit line. On other days, his duties typically include preparing forecasts of the company's future cash needs, checking bank records for errors, and administering payments on the concern's long-term debt.

But on the $30 million, the day's transactions in the money market should earn Monsanto $8,500 in interest. "A good average day," Mr. Westoby says with satisfaction.

Exhibit 8-1. MONSANTO CO.

Average Yields on Public Trades of U.S. Treasury Notes, as of August 13, 1979

Maturity Date	Average Yield on a Yearly Basis (per cent)
September 1979	10.24
October 1979	9.90
November 1979	10.05
December 1979	10.01
January 1980	10.02
February 1980	9.94
March 1980	9.91
April 1980	9.69
May 1980	9.62
June 1980	9.62
July 1980	9.58
August 1980	9.45

QUESTIONS

1. Are cash management and investment operations such as that managed by Mr. Westoby more important in times of high or of low interest rates? Why?

2. Plot the yield curve for U.S. Treasury notes as of August 13, 1979. Compare this with the "normal" yield curve. Comment on the possible reasons for any differences between these two curves.

3. Discuss the best (highest-yielding) investment strategies for a cash manager faced with (a) an upsloping yield curve; and (b) a downsloping yield curve. You may assume that whatever yield curve is involved is not expected to change in the near future and that purchased securities will be held to maturity.

4. Discuss the advantages and disadvantages of investing cash in U.S. Treasury notes versus corporate commercial paper.

5. Discuss the advantages and disadvantages to a firm such as Monsanto of a lockbox collection system with receipt locations in various parts of the country.

6. (At option of the instructor.) In light of the discussion in the article, discuss the seeming efficiency of the market for short-term securities.

Watson's Mail-Order House

*Management of Cash and Marketable Securities: The Baumol Model**

Bob Watson and his wife and children were spending part of their vacation with his parents at their home in Pittsburgh. Bob had moved from this area after college, and was now employed as a branch manager at a suburban branch of a major bank in the Midwest. His parents had run a small mail-order business from their home since his father's retirement a few years earlier. During the vacation, Bob's father had brought up an idea for improving the profits of the business.

"As you know, Bob, our mail-order business isn't really big as these things go, but it does supplement our income. We get orders throughout the month and fill them as they come in. Once we sell something, I call a supplier and have him send replacement goods to me; they usually arrive pretty quickly and the invoices are spread out over the next month. At the end of the month, your mother bills all our customers, and the money comes in pretty quickly. Once it does, we take out four per cent for profit and taxes and put the rest in the company checking account. That just covers incoming bills. The thing is, during some months we have substantial balances in the company checking account for at least part of the month. Can you think of some convenient way to put that idle cash to good use?"

*The model presented in this case originally appeared in W. J. Baumol, "The Transactions Demand for Cash: An Inventory Theoretic Approach," *Quarterly Journal of Economics*, November 1952, pp. 545-556.

Exhibit 9-1. WATSON'S MAIL-ORDER HOUSE

Time Pattern of Cash Balances

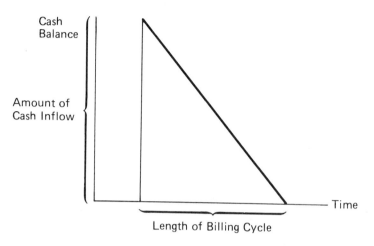

Length of Billing Cycle

This was an area in which Bob Watson had some experience. "Dad, I've had several small businessmen come into my office recently with questions like yours. Like you, they have steady outflows, but their cash comes in all at once. A very common case occurs when firms bill on terms like 'net 10 proximo'—the bill is due on the tenth of the following month. Their time pattern of cash balances books like this (see Exhibit 9-1 for Bob's first drawing).

You might consider putting this money to work by using a Negotiated Order of Withdrawal (NOW) account instead of your standard checking account. You might also consider investing part of the money temporarily in a money market fund. However, there are minimum balance requirements and fees for some NOW accounts, and similar complications for some money market funds. Instead, let's assume that rather than putting the entire cash inflow into your checking account, as you currently do, you initially put half in the checking account and half in your 5 1/4 per cent savings account. The first half of the month you use the cash in the checking account. When that runs out you take the cash you put in the savings account and transfer it to the checking account to cover bills for the rest of the month. Graphically, it looks like this for one cycle (see Exhibit 9-2 for Bob's second drawing).

This plan would require two additional transactions for you— a savings account deposit and a withdrawal—but you'd get one half month's interest on one half your cash inflow. If you

Exhibit 9-2. WATSON'S MAIL-ORDER HOUSE

Time Pattern of Cash Balances With Savings: Two Transactions

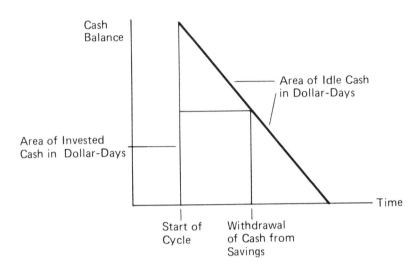

Exhibit 9-3. WATSON'S MAIL-ORDER HOUSE

Time Pattern of Cash Balances With Savings:
Three Transactions

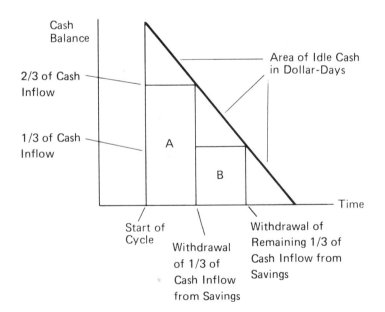

wanted to go with three transactions, you could reduce those idle cash balances still further (see Exhibit 9-3 for Bob's third drawing). Here, you get interest on two thirds of the cash inflow for one third of the month and interest on an additional one third of the cash inflow for one third of the month—the areas A and B on this diagram.

How many transactions you want to make during any month can be determined by balancing the costs of these transactions with the revenue from the interest. The formula is as follows:

$$n = \sqrt{\frac{iY}{2a}}$$

Where n is the optimum number of transactions, i is the interest rate per cash cycle, Y is the amount of the cash inflow, and a is the cost per transaction.

Bob Watson's father thought about this for a few minutes, then said, "Sounds good to me, Bob. Could you do a few examples? Our sales are quite seasonal, and here is an estimate of these volumes for the next few months (see Exhibit 9-4). You can estimate the cost per transaction as $5 for my time, wear and tear on the car, gasoline, and the like."

Exhibit 9-4. WATSON'S MAIL-ORDER HOUSE

Estimate of Sales for Months of 10/80 to 3/81

Month	Sales in Dollars
Oct. 1980	36,000
Nov. 1980	44,000
Dec. 1980	30,000
Jan. 1981	24,000
Feb. 1981	21,600
Mar. 1981	19,200

QUESTIONS

1. Develop a cash management strategy for Watson's Mail-Order House for each of the months of November 1980 through April 1981 using the cash management model described by Bob Watson. Be sure to calculate the optimal number of transactions

during each month (this must be an integer), the amount of each initial deposit, the amount of each withdrawal, and the transactions dates during each month.

2. Calculate the additional income (interest less transaction costs) that would accrue to Watson's Mail-Order House from using the model for these six months.

3. Suppose that instead of using the 5 1/4 per cent savings account as his repository for idle funds, Bob's father elects to use a money market fund yielding 14 per cent per year. The fund, however, will only accept deposits or withdrawals in even multiples of $500; Bob's father would incur a $7.50 cost per transaction if such a fund were used. Redo Question 1 using these new parameters; indicate the difference in total profits over the six-month period between this strategy and the use of the savings account.

4. (At option of the instructor.) Would a much larger firm (say, with monthly sales of $100 million) with the same cash flow pattern (lumped inflows and even outflows) and a cash cycle of six months probably use the cash management model outlined in the case? Why or why not?

The Polyurethane Company

Management of Cash and Marketable Securities:
The Miller-Orr Model

The Polyurethane Company was the largest division of a middle-sized chemical manufacturer. The company made chemicals for the production of polyurethane foam. Polyurethane foam is made by mixing chemicals together under controlled conditions. The reaction is exothermic (gives off heat). The type of chemicals used determines the consistency of the foam produced; hard or soft, with large or small bubbles. Hard, large-bubbled urethane foams were often used as insulation materials; softer, small-bubbled foams, as shoe soles. The most common use of urethane foam, however, was in cushions and mattresses. Here, the largest-selling urethane chemical, 80/20 toluene diisocyanate (the 80/20 indicates the mix of monomers), was mixed with another chemical and extruded in long, rectangular "buns," which were then cut into convenient sizes, usually using a hot wire system. The foam produced was soft and large-bubbled and ideal for comfort applications. The Polyurethane Company in the early 1980s sold about $200 million worth of 80/20 toluene diisocyanate and similar chemicals yearly.

In middle-sized firms such as The Polyurethane Company, low- and middle-level managers often "wear many hats": they do several jobs, which in a larger firm would be handled by specialists. Thomas Charles who had an undergraduate degree and an MBA from a large land-grant university, was the company's assistant credit manager, accounts receivable manager, cash reporter, and forecaster. Also (but less frequently), he

51

assisted the accounting department in computing breakeven points, performed accounting functions, and helped the firm's planning department with statistical analysis. When the firm's finance department moved to offices in a new building, Charles was heard to remark, somewhat jovially, "I hope my office isn't near the boiler; they'll have me shoveling coal, too!"

One of Charles' duties, that of cash forecaster for the company, had become increasingly important. A sample of one of Charles' forecasts is presented as Exhibit 10-1. The firm had just undertaken a program of active management of its cash asset, and Charles' forecasts of daily cash flows were used, along with similar forecasts from other parts of the firm, in making short-term investment decisions. For example, if these forecasts showed that the firm had excess cash early in a week that would not be needed until later in that week, short-term securities (usually Treasury bills) would be purchased to earn interest on the idle cash until it was needed. Because The Polyurethane Company was the firm's largest division, Charles' forecasts were critical to the process. Charles, however, was not happy with the accuracy of his forecasts of daily cash flow. If his forecasts were in error, the cash manager's plans had to be changed; securities sometimes had to be sold before the planned sale date. This was inconvenient and expensive.

Exhibit 10-1. THE POLYURETHANE COMPANY

Forecast of Daily Cash Flows (Book Balances) For the Business Week of 1/11/82 to 1/15/82 (Rounded Thousands of Dollars)

	Monday 1/11/82	Tuesday 1/12/82	Wednesday 1/13/82	Thursday 1/14/82	Friday 1/15/82
Starting cash balance	200	827	387	(53)	174
Receipts	1667	600	600	1267	1100
Total funds	1867	1427	987	1214	1274
Disbursements	1040	1040	1040	1040	1040
Cash balance, end of day	827	387	(53)	174	234
Desired cash balance	140	140	140	140	140
Surplus or (deficit)	687	247	(193)	34	94

Charles found the current inaccuracy of these forecasts quite perplexing. The company's sales were somewhat seasonal, but by assuming an average collection period of forty days, and by using the company's forecast of monthly sales, Charles could make fairly accurate forecasts of monthly flows. The difficulty was in forecasting daily flows within the month. Charles had searched for patterns in these daily flows in several ways. He had examined flows shortly after the tenth and twenty-fifth of the month, under the hypothesis that some customers write checks on these dates (a common practice some years ago); he did not find any obviously heavy inflows, however. He examined the receipts from the company's lockbox, and found no pattern, aside from the inordinately large receipts on Mondays. This "Monday effect" was caused by checks received in the bank's mail on both Saturday and Monday being credited on a book (but not cleared) basis to the company's account on Monday. He ran regressions looking for weekly and daily forecasting tools, but the significance levels of these regressions were minimal. In short, Charles struck out.

In desperation, he talked the problem over with his friend and golfing partner, David Feldstein. "Tom," Feldstein said, "has it occurred to you that except for the lumping of book receipts on Mondays and the seasonality among months all this movement might be random? If that's true, all this churning of cash and marketable securities on the basis of your forecasts is counterproductive. Maybe what is needed is a new short-term

Exhibit 10-2. THE POLYURETHANE COMPANY

Changes in Cleared Bank Balances (Cleared Daily Net Cash Flows) Month of January 1982 (Business Days Only; Rounded Thousands of Dollars)

Monday	Tuesday	Wednesday	Thursday	Friday
				1/1/82 Holiday
1/4/82 (445)	1/5/82 (137)	1/6/82 376	1/7/82 (34)	1/8/82 445
1/11/82 (479)	1/12/82 274	1/13/82 (96)	1/14/82 294	1/15/82 501
1/18/82 239	1/19/82 34	1/20/82 171	1/21/82 308	1/22/82 (342)
1/25/82 (205)	1/26/82 (103)	1/27/82 (117)	1/28/82 616	1/29/82 (137)

investment strategy. Why don't you come up with one and show management how it applies? The Financial Vice-President isn't unsophisticated; a few quick-and-dirty statistical tests and an example analysis should convince him."

Charles thought about this for a time and decided to give it a try; after all, he thought, the alternative to a pattern is randomness. He decided to use as his sample data changes in the company's cleared bank balance from the previous month (these data are presented in Exhibit 10–2). As his cash management decision model, he decided to use the Miller-Orr model,* which assumes that daily cash flows are normally distributed, uncorrelated from day to day, and that the distribution of daily cash flows is stationary over time.

QUESTIONS

1. Until his present analysis effort, Charles had been dealing with the company's book cash balances. Such book balances are calculated by recording cash receipts when they are deposited (but not cleared) and recording disbursement checks as they are written. From a cash management standpoint, why is it better to focus on cleared, rather than book, balances? What floats are ignored in using book balances for cash management purposes?

2. Calculate the mean and standard deviation of the daily cleared cash flows of The Polyurethane Company for the month of January 1982. Consider only business days.

3. Perform a goodness-of-fit test comparing the company's daily cash flows to those that would be expected if these flows were normally distributed. Although the Kolmogorov-Smirnov test is better for small samples, you may use a chi-square test for the purposes of this case. Consider only business days and use six outcome ranges:

1. Cash flow less than ($500,000).
2. Cash flow between ($499,999) and ($250,000).
3. Cash flow between ($249,999) and $0.
4. Cash flow between $0 and $250,000.
5. Cash flow between $250,001 and $500,000.
6. Cash flow over $500,000.

Ignore the usual requirement that the expected frequency in each range must be at least five to use chi-square.

*See M. H. Miller and D. Orr, "A Model of the Demand for Money by Firms," *Quarterly Journal of Economics*, August 1966, pp. 413–435.

4. Perform a correlation test to see whether the company's cleared daily cash flows during the business days of January 1982 were serially correlated (and thus whether the cash flow distributions were independent from day to day). A student's t test based on the Pearson product-moment correlation coefficient will be sufficient.

5. If the data are normally distributed and serially uncorrelated, the major assumptions of the Miller-Orr cash management model are fulfilled. Assuming that The Polyurethane Company was forced to keep a $140,000 compensating balance, that brokerage fees were $100 per transaction, that the initial cleared cash balance was $500,000, and that the firm could earn 12 per cent per year by investing surplus funds in Treasury bills, calculate the upper control limit and the return point for the Miller-Orr model. Show graphically and describe the time pattern of the company's cash balances (cleared) for January 1982 had the model been used (ignore cash flow effects from transaction costs and earnings associated with the model). Calculate the average cash balance that would result.

6. (At the option of the instructor.) Contrast the assumptions of the Baumol (EOQ) and Miller-Orr cash management models. Give some typical circumstances under which each is likely to be most applicable.

Plastics Manufacturing, Inc.

Accounts Receivable Management: Terms of Sale

Plastics Manufacturing, Inc., with headquarters in Houston, Texas, was a major producer of plastic resins in early 1978. The production of raw plastic from chemical feedstocks was a complex technical process requiring significant capital investments. In this process, the molecules of the feedstocks (such as ethylene) were combined into longer, chainlike molecules. These larger molecules were solid and gave the plastic its strength. Once his process had been performed, the plastic was granulated (made into small pellets) and packaged for shipment. Packages ranged in size from fifty-pound bags to large railroad hopper cars.

Although the number of producers of any particular type of plastic was generally fairly small (between two and ten), the number of buyers of a plastic were several thousand. These users ground up and heated the plastic pellets (turning the plastic back into a liquid), formed the plastic into desired shapes, then cooled it back to a solid state. These operations required machinery that was relatively simple and required only a small capital investment. As a consequence, many of these operations were performed by small plastic molders—firms that took contracts from end-use manufacturers to produce quantities of plastic parts from the raw plastic pellets. The end-use manufacturer generally provided the mold for a specific part, which was installed on the plastic molder's equipment. After the job was complete, this mold was returned to the end-use manufacturer.

Because these plastic molding operations required only a small amount of capital, and because only a moderate amount of expertise was required to run such an operation, the profitability of plastic molders was generally very small. There were a great many of them in most areas of the country and they competed for the business of the end-use manufacturers. Further, if they tried to price their services with any large profit margin, the end-use manufacturers, who were generally larger firms, could purchase the plastic molding equipment and do the molding themselves, and many had done so. As a consequence, many plastic molders tended to remain thinly capitalized firms with poor liquidity and thus were poor credit risks.

It was the job of Jack Bryan, credit manager for Plastics Manufacturing, to decide which of the firms that had applied to his firm for credit to buy materials would be allowed to purchase on a credit basis. For the end-use manufacturers who did their own plastic moldings, this was an easy task, because most of these firms were quite creditworthy. Many of the plastic molding job shops, however, were in too poor a financial position to meet the firm's credit standards. Further, many of the larger and somewhat more creditworthy plastic molders required extended terms—terms of sale beyond Plastics Manufacturing's standard terms of sale of net thirty days. Such extended terms were a financing method for these plastic molders; taking longer to pay for purchases lowered their required funds from other sources to support their operations. It had been Plastics Manufacturing's policy in the past to deny such terms and consequently lose the patronage of these potential purchasers. With this policy in mind, Frank Blanko, the firm's general sales manager, approached Jack Bryan with a proposal.

"Jack, I've gone over our recent market survey, and there are quite a number of potential customers who require these extended terms of sale. Although some of them can't be justified, we have confirmed that some are already getting these terms from other plastics suppliers. As you know, we can meet these terms of sale to these specific customers without changing our terms to other customers and without violating the law under the 'meeting competition in good faith' provisions of the antitrust statutes. Considering only customers of this type, where we could be meeting competition, I've prepared a chart." (See Exhibit 11-1 for Blanko's chart.)

"I'd appreciate it if you could do some analysis here from a credit standpoint. We have enough plant capacity to handle all this volume. If it looks as if we should grant any of these extended terms, we go to the treasurer and propose a policy change."

Exhibit 11-1. PLASTICS MANUFACTURING, INC.

Expected Additional Yearly Sales from Meeting
Terms Competition

Additional Terms Allowed in Days	Expected Additional Sales Per Year in Dollars	Number of Additional Customers in Group
30	4,000,000	40
60	7,500,000	75
90	1,125,000	15
120	500,000	15
150	200,000	10

Bryan knew that the marginal profits that could be obtained from these accounts had to be balanced against the costs of maintaining the accounts: credit administration costs, accounts receivable carrying costs, and expected bad debt costs. Because each of the new accounts involved substantial sales volume, he decided to estimate a relatively large amount per account for credit administration costs: $350 per year. This amount was to cover transportation costs for credit personnel to visit the new accounts, additional expenses of correspondence with the new accounts, and the like. He intended to use the firm's 10 per cent per year investment opportunity rate for accounts receivable carrying costs with accounts receivable investment expressed in sales dollars. In estimating expected bad debt expense, Bryan knew that the longer the extended terms required, the less liquid and creditworthy the new account was likely to be. Consequently, he decided to assign a 1.5 per cent probability of default during each year to new accounts requiring thirty additional days extended terms, 3 per cent to those requiring sixty additional days, 7 per cent to those requiring ninety additional days, 20 per cent to those requiring 120 additional days, and 40 per cent to those requiring 150 additional days. He also decided to assume a zero recovery in all defaults. The actual amount of the expected loss, of course, would depend on the average exposure of the firm to the new accounts. For example, using a 360-day year, for those new accounts requiring thirty additional days, if these accounts pay promptly on these new terms, invoices to these accounts will be outstanding for a total of sixty days, or one sixth of a year. The average exposure would then be (1/6) ($4,000,000), or $666.667. Bryan decided to assume that on the average the new accounts would pay fifteen days beyond their granted terms. He also had available his own firm's current financial statements (see Exhibits 11-2 and 11-3).

Exhibit 11-2. PLASTICS MANUFACTURING, INC.

Balance Sheet as of 12/31/77 (Rounded Thousands of Dollars)

Cash	$ 5,470	Due to banks, short	
Mar. securities	1,157	term	$ 4,629
Accts. receivable	26,931	Accounts payable	15,044
Inventories	23,880	Accrued income taxes	2,630
Prepaid expenses	2,420	Due on long-term debt	2,525
Total current assets	$ 59,858	Other current liabilities	6,838
		Total current liabilities	$ 31,666
Property, plant,			
and equipment		Long-term debt	21,882
less accumulated			
depreciation	41,554	Net worth	51,652
Other assets	3,788	Total liabilities and	
Total assets	$105,200	net worth	$105,200

Exhibit 11-3. PLASTICS MANUFACTURING, INC.

Income Statement for Fiscal 1977 (Rounded Thousands of Dollars)

Sales	$263,000
Cost of goods sold[1]	193,305
Gross margin on sales	69,695
Selling, administrative, and	
general expenses[2]	48,392
Earnings before taxes	21,303
Taxes	9,906
Earnings after taxes	$ 11,397

[1] Includes all variable costs of manufacturing, direct labor, direct materials, etc.

[2] Includes all fixed costs of the firm.

QUESTIONS

1. Calculate the expected marginal profits and additional credit costs of granting the required extended term to each group of customers.

2. To which customer classes should extended terms be granted? Why?

3. (At option of the instructor.) Discuss the advantages and disadvantages to the firm of changing the terms of sale to all customers to sixty days rather than only to those customers that request it. Include in your response the probable reaction of competitors to this maneuver.

Universal Chemical Products

Accounts Receivable Management: Profitability and Credit Policy

Stephanie Knight, the general credit manager for Universal Chemical Products, had responsibility for (among other things) formulating the credit policies of the firm. These policies were then implemented by the credit analysts, each of whom handled several hundred individual accounts.

Recently, Mrs. Knight had been considering adjusting the firm's credit policy to take into account differences between the products sold by the three divisions of the firm. Mrs. Knight was concerned about two important aspects of credit policy: the riskiness of the accounts that are granted credit and the type and intensity of collection techniques used by the credit analysts. Analysts judged the riskiness of accounts by their standing on the "five Cs of credit": the account's character, capacity, capital, collateral, and conditions. With respect to collection techniques, the analysts could be aggressive and try for quick collections (which often irritated customers) or lax and allow a little more leniency in payments. The firm's credit policy in these areas affected both sales and costs. A loose policy of granting credit to risky accounts and allowing leniency in payments would generate more sales, but increased the costs of bad debts (because of more defaults) and of carrying receivables (because customers took more time to pay). A stringent policy of declining credit to risky accounts and vigorously pursuing accounts for payment would cut costs but reduce sales as well.

In early 1980, the credit policy of Universal Chemical Products was to treat accounts from each of the three divisions similarly; the same standards of riskiness and collection techniques were used for all. For example, to expedite shipments to new customers, the firm had a policy of granting an initial amount of credit to any new account without further investigation on the basis of the account's Dun and Bradstreet rating. The amounts granted were the same regardless of the division from which the account was purchasing. This policy had been inherited by Mrs. Knight from her predecessor as general credit manager. However, she had succeeded in upgrading the average education of many of the credit analysts employed by the firm, and she believed that a policy more sensitive to the differences among the product lines sold by the three divisions could now be successfully implemented.

All three divisions had their own plants and produced chemical products from raw materials for different markets. The Polymerized Materials Group made plastics from raw materials. The Foam Product Group made chemicals for producing mat-

Exhibit 12-1. UNIVERSAL CHEMICAL PRODUCTS

Statement of Income by Product Group (for Fiscal 1979, Rounded Thousands of Dollars)

	Polymerized Materials	Foam Products	Agricultural Products	Firm as a Whole
Sales	$211,019	$156,207	$101,602	$468,828
Sales salaries	6,331	4,686	3,048	14,065
Materials[1]	109,730	86,226	54,459	250,415
Service staff	2,110	1,562	1,016	4,688
Depreciation[2]	25,322	7,810	7,112	40,244
Direct labor +OH	27,432	21,557	13,615	62,604
Research & development	10,551	3,124	8,128	21,803
Indirect OH[3]	16,878	12,489	8,139	37,506
Earnings before taxes	12,665	18,753	6,085	37,503
Taxes	5,699	8,439	2,738	16,876
Earnings after taxes	$ 6,966	$ 10,314	$ 3,347	$ 20,627
EBT/sales	6.0%	12.0%	6.0%	8.0%

[1] Feedstocks and other direct materials used in making products for sale.
[2] Depreciation on plants; sum-of-years-digits method.
[3] Headquarters expense, computer expense, depreciation on headquarters buildings; allocated on the basis of per cent of sales. All other group entries are allocated on the basis of actual group expenses.

tresses, pillows, and the like. The Agricultural Products Group made farm products. The plants used by Foam Products and Agricultural Products Groups were several years old, whereas the Polymerized Materials Group had recently completed a new facility. The three groups also had different policies with regard to research and development; the Agricultural Products and Polymerized Materials Groups maintained fairly active programs, but the research and development activity in the Foam Products group was quite limited. All three groups paid their salesmen on a straight commission basis and maintained service staffs to advise customers who had problems using the firm's products. These service staffs were paid on a straight salary basis and commonly had considerable free time. In order to analyze the profitability of the three divisions, Mrs. Knight obtained statements of income, generated by the accounting department, for the three groups and the firm as a whole (see Exhibit 12-1). She knew that all three divisions had some spare production capacity. She wanted to set the firm's credit policy guidelines to stimulate sales in divisions where these would be highly profitable on a marginal basis, but be more stringent where marginal profits were lower.

QUESTIONS

1. Restate the group statements of income presented in Exhibit 12-1 to reflect only the marginal expenses and revenues (those that would change proportionately with changes in credit policy). Compute the ratio of "profit per dollar of marginal sales" (income before taxes divided by sales). Financial decisions, of course, deal only with such marginal costs and revenues.

2. Where should the firm's credit policy be most strict? Most loose? Why? How does this differ from the same conclusions based on the original income statements by groups? Why?

3. (At option of the instructor.) Suppose that the plants of the divisions were being depreciated by the units-of-production method instead of the sum-of-the-years-digits method. How would this change your analysis in Question 1?

Industrial Materials, Inc.

Accounts Receivable Management: Credit Decision Systems

In the middle of 1975, Ms. Jane Alistair was employed by Industrial Materials, Inc., as credit manager. Industrial Materials, Inc. had headquarters in San Francisco and was a supplier of various common industrial products used in manufacturing (screws, bolts, flanges, and other metal parts). Ms. Alistair had been credit manager of the firm for about two years, having previously served in a similar position with another firm. Over the past few months, she had become increasingly aware of the problems with the firm's decision-making system for credit applicants.

The decision-making system used by Industrial Materials, Inc. was a traditional one used by many firms that grant credit to industrial customers. In this system, information about a credit applicant was gathered from various sources: Dun and Bradstreet, other suppliers, banks, directly from the applicant, and so forth. This information usually includes the firm's history, record of payments to other suppliers, financial position, and so forth. The credit analyst then looked at these data and made a decision regarding a credit limit for the applicant. The applicant was allowed to have up to this amount outstanding on an account, provided that the account was not past due. The intent of the credit limit was to enable the supplier to sell the applicant materials on competitive credit terms while keeping the amount owed (known as exposure in the credit business) at a level commensurate with the applicant's credit worthiness. The setting of credit limits in this way was based on the judgment of the credit analyst regarding the applicant's credit worthiness from the collected data. The credit limits set in this way were thus, to some extent, arbitrary. This caused problems between the credit and sales departments; because the sales department always wanted higher credit lines to facilitate sales, it continually questioned the judgment of the analysts. Ms. Alistair believed this process caused quite a bit of friction between her department and others, so she looked for another way to approach the setting of credit limits. One approach she was considering was formulized credit limits (one such formula is provided in Appendix A of this case).

In the formulized approach, the credit limit is obtained by summing the contribution of a series of factors. These factors are supposed to account for all the significant measures of the applicant's ability and propensity to pay, and thus the applicant's credit worthiness. Such systems can use any data that is believed to be important and can be quantified; the person(s) originally developing the formulized credit limit system decide what should go in it and how important each factor is (reflected in the weight given to the factor in determining the credit limit). One of the advantages of a formulized system is that each analyst, utilizing this system on a particular account, will generally arrive at the same credit limit (although there may be some ambiguity because some factors may require the analyst's judgment).

As a case in point, Ms. Alistair wanted to compare the results of a credit line for a credit applicant set by the judgmental system (outlined in the Appendix) with that set by one of the credit analysts working in her department. She selected as an example California General Manufacturing Company, which had recently been presented to her department by the sales force as a possible future customer. California General Manufacturing had been founded in the 1950s and had grown rapidly, having sales of more than $4 million for fiscal 1979 (see Exhibits 13-1, 13-2, and 13-3 for California General's balance sheets, income statements, and payments to the trade.) The firm manufactured a diverse line of proprietary items, such as small medical instruments and electrical connectors, and also performed some plastic molding and machine shop work for other firms. The sales force had estimated potential sales to California General Manufacturing at $150,000 per month, and were upset that Tom Bowen had set a credit limit of only $100,000 for the applicant. When Ms. Alistair had inquired about Bowen's thinking here, she got the following response:

"Jane, here's how I analyze the account. It is clear from the financial statements that the firm is well situated from a marketing standpoint and is growing rapidly. It's liquidity is excellent and so is its debt position. These are the good points. However, the marginal profitability of the products we would sell them is only moderate, and I'm concerned about their payments to the trade. Although the ability to pay is there, based on their liquidity, there is some slowness to the trade, particularly to bigger suppliers, which is what we would be. The account is certainly safe from a bad debt standpoint, but we should expect slowness in payment. Consequently, I've set a credit line that I believe is a compromise of the considerations."

Exhibit 13-1. INDUSTRIAL MATERIALS, INC.

Balance Sheets of California General Manufacturing Co. for
Fiscal Years Ending 4/30/73 to 4/30/75

Year Ending	4/30/73	4/30/74	4/30/75
Cash	$ 16,295	$ 124,839	$ 125,417
Notes receivable	—	—	25,112
Accounts receivable	572,146	485,294	481,302
Inventory	313,445	531,672	449,129
Certificates of deposit	93,750	93,750	93,750
Prepaid expenses	11,037	15,739	13,991
Total current assets	1,006,673	1,251,294	1,188,701
Fixed assets less accumulated depreciation	652,712	718,864	690,552
Other assets	29,325	35,996	48,848
Total assets	1,688,710	2,006,154	1,928,101
Notes payable	56,250	—	42,000
Accounts payable	340,381	435,335	229,208
Accruals	85,766	118,362	118,820
Income taxes payable	11,972	106,327	55,508
Current portion, L.T.D.	30,000	30,000	30,000
Total current liabilities	524,369	690,024	475,536
Long-term debt	315,000	285,000	255,000
Deferred income taxes	11,842	12,592	15,591
Common stock	187,950	187,950	187,950
Capital surplus	132,395	132,395	132,395
Retained earnings	517,154	698,193	861,629
Owner's equity	837,499	1,018,538	1,181,974
Total liabilities and owner's equity	$1,688,710	$2,006,154	$1,928,101

Exhibit 13-2. INDUSTRIAL MATERIALS, INC.

Income Statements for California General Manufacturing
Company for Fiscal Years Ending 4/30/73 to 4/30/75

Year Ending	4/30/73	4/30/74	4/30/75
Net sales	$2,971,691	$4,112,662	$4,626,257
Cost of goods sold	2,139,618	2,961,120	3,423,430
Gross margin on sales	832,073	1,151,547	1,202,827
Selling and other expenses	570,305	782,364	906,336
Other income or (expense)	7,265	7,982	8,001
Net profit before taxes	269,033	377,165	340,492
Taxes	139,897	196,126	177,056
Earnings after taxes	$ 129,136	$ 181,039	$ 163,436

Exhibit 13-3. INDUSTRIAL MATERIALS, INC.

Trade Clearance for California General Manufacturing Co. as
of early 1975

Supplier No.	Highest Credit Extended	Now Owing	Now Past Due	Term of Sale	Payment Record
089	$ 400	$ 200	0	Not Given	Prompt
072	800	0	0	1% 10 Net 30	Prompt, discounts
111	1,500	100	0	Net 30	Slow, 30 days
109	4,200	800	0	Net 30	Prompt
007	15,000	4,500	3,000	Net 30	Slow, 15–30 days
012	$75,000	$75,000	$57,000	Net 30	Slow, 60 days

QUESTIONS

1. Compute the credit limit for California General Manufacturing Co. based on the formulized system outlined in the Appendix. Contrast this result with the credit limit set by Tom
Bowen.

2. What factors were considered by Tom Bowen that are not
explicitly included in the formulized approach outlined in the
Appendix? What factors are included in the formulized approach
that were not considered by Tom Bowen?

3. Outline some advantages and disadvantages to Industrial Materials, Inc., of using the formulized approach to setting credit limits.

4. (At option of the instructor.) The factors included and weights assigned in the formulized method indicate the opinions of those developing the system about what is important in the credit granting decision and what is not. Critique the system outlined in the Appendix on this basis, keeping in mind that the most important measures of credit worthiness cited in most texts are debt and liquidity measures.

APPENDIX A

A Formulized Credit Limit System*

This system is based on percents of tangible net worth. The contributions from each factor are summed and multiplied times the applicant firm's tangible net worth in dollars to obtain the credit limit in dollars. Analysis is based on the last fiscal year's data. There are thirteen factors in the system:

Factor 1: Initial contribution. This is the applicant's "basic" credit line, equal to 10 per cent of net worth.

Factor 2: Percent of applicant's cost of sales sold (excluding labor) to be furnished by supplier. This gives some idea of the bargaining power the supplier will have in credit dealings.

Percent of Cost of Sales, Excluding Labor, To Be Furnished by Supplier	Contribution to Credit Limit
under 25%	0
25% to 50%	+5% of TNW
over 50%	+10% of TNW

Factor 3: Pay habit. This measure is based on the applicant's payments to the trade.

Payments	Contribution to Credit Limit
Generally discounts when available or pays promptly where terms are net	+10% of TNW
Pays promptly but does not discount	+5% of TNW
Pays "as agreed" or no experience	0
Occasionally late in payments	–2.5% of TNW
Consistently late in payments	–5% of TNW

*The basic system used here is presented in "Credit Limits Established by Formula and Computer," Occasional Paper, Credit Research Foundation, Inc. It is used by a division of a major U.S. corporation.

Factor 4: Years in business. This factor is based on the idea that older firms are less likely to fail.

Number of Years in Business	Contribution to Credit Limit
under 3	0
3 to 10	+2.5 of TNW
over 10	+5% of TNW

Factor 5: Profit margin. This factor encompasses the concept that profitable firms are more likely to have the cash to pay promptly. For each one per cent of pretax profit (loss) margin, the applicant receives 0.2 per cent of tangible net worth as a contribution (deduction) to the credit limit. Profit margin is defined as earnings before taxes divided by net sales.

Factor 6: Current ratio. This, of course, is a liquidity measure.

Current Ratio	Contribution to Credit Limit
2.00 and over	+10% of TNW
1.25 to 1.99	+5% of TNW
0.75 to 1.24	0
less than 0.75	−5% of TNW

Factor 7: Quick ratio. This is another liquidity measure. This ratio is calculated on a restrictive basis in that only cash, short-term marketable securities, and net receivables are in the numerator.

Quick Ratio	Contribution to Credit Limit
2.00 and over	+15% of TNW
1.00 to 1.99	+10% of TNW
0.80 to 0.99	+5% of TNW
0.50 to 0.79	0
less than 0.50	−5% of TNW

Factor 8: Ratio of current liabilities to inventory. This is another liquidity-type ratio, with low ratios representing high liquidity.

Part II: Current Asset Management

Ratio	Contribution to Credit Limit
Less than 0.65	+10% of TNW
0.65 to 0.99	0
1.00 and over	–5% of TNW

Factor 9: Ratio of inventory to net working capital. This is an inventory management ratio and is assumed to go through an optimal range.

Ratio	Contribution to Credit Limit
less than 0.25	–5%of TNW
0.25 to 0.49	0
0.50 to 0.99	+5% of TNW
more than 0.99	–5% of TNW

Factor 10: Debt ratio. Ratios of this sort measure the safety of the applicant's debt. This debt ratio is defined as tangible net worth plus subordinated debt divided by unsubordinated debt.

Ratio	Contribution to Credit Limit
2.00 and over	+10% of TNW
1.00 to 1.99	+5% of TNW
less than 1.00	–5% of TNW

Factor 11: Receivables management. This ratio measures the applicant's management of receivables. The applicant's average collection period in days in first computed (year-end accounts receivable divided by sales times 360). A contribution of 0.1 per cent of tangible net worth is given to the applicant's credit line for each day that the applicant's average collection period is less than the terms of sale that the applicant grants plus thirty days.

Factor 12: Inventory turnover. This ratio, equal to inventory divided into cost of sales, is supposed to measure the applicant's efficiency in managing this asset. It is assumed to go through an optimal range.

Ratio	Contribution to Credit Limit
less than 5.00	0
5.00 to 9.99	+5% of TNW
10.00 to 30.00	+10% of TNW
more than 30.00	0

Factor 13: Analyst's judgment and other considerations. This allows the analyst to include any data not included in the other factors. In some systems, this adjustment is limited to a certain contribution.

RZW Electronic Parts Co.

Inventory Management Models (1)

Ed Rogers had been an amateur radio operator for many years and was aware of the problems that "ham" radio operators were having in obtaining parts for their projects. Many of them were tinkerers who liked to build and improve their own equipment. Most magazines directed at the amateur radio market had several build-it-yourself (known in the hobby as "homebrew") projects in each issue. In the early 1960s, it was common to find a shop or two in any town that carried inventories of such parts and sold amateur radio, citizens' band (CB), and audio equipment. Many such shops could advise customers on parts selection; if the store was out of one part, they could suggest a substitute. However, the years brought some changes in businesses of this type. Chain stores sold electronic equipment and provided substantial competition; department and discount stores began to trade more heavily in audio equipment; the CB boom shifted interest away from amateur radio. Some electronics shops went out of business, but most adapted to these market changes by dropping their parts and amateur radio lines to concentrate on CB and audio equipment. Hams could obtain some of the more common parts from the chain stores selling electronic equipment, such as the Radio Shack chain, but many other parts necessary for their projects (variable capacitors, coils, and the like) were not stocked by such stores. Although parts of this type were listed in catalogs of some commercial electronics supply houses, they did not like to service small orders. Attempts to obtain parts from these sources resulted in high prices and substantial delays. As a result, a number of small parts specialty houses serving the ham market had been established by the mid-1970s. These businesses bought parts from manufacturers or commercial supply houses, held them in inventory, and sold them to hams in small quantities on a mail-order basis. Ed Rogers and several other local hams ran such a business on a part-time basis. Rogers was in charge of ordering the parts from suppliers. The other partners were in charge of handling the merchandise when it was received and of filling orders. Inventory was stored in bins in the basement of one of the partners. Once a week, Rogers checked the inventories stored in each bin. If the supply on hand of any part seemed low, he would then order a sufficient number of parts to fill the bin. These parts generally took about two weeks to arrive and could be ordered in just about any quantity.

One day after checking the bins, Rogers was having a few beers with George Bradford, another partner in the venture. Bradford was in charge of filling the orders as received. "Ed, I think we may have an inventory problem." Bradford said "Some of the bins always seem to be full, but we seem to be out of some parts half of the time. As I see it, a major reason people order parts from us is that we provide prompt service, which we can't do if we are out of stock; yet we don't want to incur too high costs. We can always change the bin sizes if we need to. What do you think?"

Exhibit 14-1.   RZW ELECTRONIC PARTS CO.

Demand and Cost Figures for Ten Parts

	Part No.	Demand per Mo. (units)	Cost per Part
1-15-mmf. variable capacitor	011	10	$1.05
1/4-inch slug-tuned coil form	027	128	2.10
50-250-mmf. trimmer capacitor	031	87	.85
1/2-inch ceramic coil form	033	72	2.20
10-megohm wire-wound potentiometer	047	206	.75
80-meter crystal, novice band	050	27	5.25
MOSFET rf amplifier, RCA SK3065	072	84	3.10
510-mmf. polystyrene capacitor	075	13	.60
2.5-mh. rf choke	089	21	4.75
1-mf. tantalum capacitor	107	32	1.60

Rogers had not been aware of this problem and decided to give the matter some thought. The next day, he selected ten parts the firm kept in stock and developed a chart of demand and cost (see Exhibit 14–1). He decided to estimate the cost of placing and receiving an order (his time to fill out the required forms, mailing costs, the time of those who unpacked the order, and so on) at $5.00 per order and inventory carrying costs at 12 per cent per year.

QUESTIONS

1. Calculate the economic order quantity for each of the ten parts. Note that the order quantity must be an integer.
2. Calculate the required level of safety stock for each item. Use the formula:

$$A = 1.85\sqrt{LS}$$

Where A is the safety stock in units, L is the average lead time from order to delivery, and S is the usage per period.

3. Calculate the average inventory in units for each part if the order quantities and safety stocks previously calculated are used.
4. One method of deciding when to order each part on the basis of the economic order quantity model is called the order point system. Here, the partners whose job it is to fill incoming orders and to put new orders in the bins would keep running totals of the quantity in each bin. When the order point was reached, a new order for the part would be placed. Calculate order points for each of the ten parts.
5. How is the EOQ order point system an improvement over Rogers' "look in the bin" system? Discuss differences with respect to cost and customer service.
6. (At option of the instructor.) It is implied in Exhibit 14–1 that there are no quantity discounts for the purchase of various amounts of any part. Suppose the price schedule for Part Number 033 was actually:

Quantity ordered	1 to 9	10 to 49	50 to 249	over 249
Manufacturer's price per part	$3.00	$2.50	$2.20	$2.10

How does this affect the EOQ? Why? What is the new EOQ?

Railroad Signaling Equipment Co.

Inventory Management Models (2)

Railroad Signaling Equipment Company (RSE) produced a diverse line of switching and signaling parts for the railroad and mass transit industries. RSE produced both original equipment and replacement parts. Switching and signaling products, (such as track switches, block control signals, and so on) were used as part of track systems to direct on-track vehicles and to control their speeds. Also included were products to direct the flow of off-track vehicles at railroad crossings, such as crossing gates and "train coming" signal lights. The manufacture and sale of switching and signaling products was complicated by an important technological factor: the mix of old and new equipment in use. Much of the railroad equipment in use was installed in the 1930s and before, but some was of much more recent design and manufacture. Equipment designed in the 1920s might require manual operation but would be electronically controlled if designed in the 1970s. Because it was RSE's policy to stock replacement parts for all equipment that had been manufactured by the firm since 1910, stocks of tens of thousands of different parts, representing technologies in different periods, were required. These replacement parts were often demanded on short notice by the railroads if a critical piece of equipment failed. Thus, the management of inventory investment was a major concern for RSE.

Donald Kyle, a business graduate of an eastern university, was employed in the firm's finance department. In late 1979, the

Exhibit 15-1. RAILROAD SIGNALING EQUIPMENT CO.

Statistics for Parts Produced on Reserved Milling Machine Number 62

Part No.	Out-of-Pocket Setup Cost	Out-of-Pocket Cost per Unit	Usage per Year (Units)	Production Capacity of Reserved Machine per Year for this Part if Used Continuously (Units)
8752A	$ 21	$ 1.85	200	25,000
11156B	53	5.06	50	5,000
8457A	107	0.57	10,000	60,000
4372C	25	10.62	750	10,000
8045A	85	5.57	5,000	100,000
7524B	10	20.62	300	2,500
6210M	15	10.85	1,500	10,000
2111D	$ 41	$ 4.68	650	20,000

firm launched a program to reduce inventories, both of finished goods (replacement and original equipment) and work-in-process. The program was prompted by the high short-term interest rates in effect at the time. The prime rate was more than 15 per cent, and RSE wanted to determine if some savings in inventory carrying costs could be achieved. In an attempt to ascertain the company's current practices regarding some of its work-in-process inventories, Kyle had arranged a meeting with William Langdon, one of the firm's production supervisors.

"Sometimes production and inventory considerations are connected, Don," Langdon had said. "This isn't a retail business. We have a lot of specialized products, and we make parts for them ourselves. We often turn some of our own screws. However, there is one class of parts I can think of where you might help us out in production scheduling and reduce inventories at the same time. We have several milling machines set aside to make parts for other operations. When we become short on a part for a particular product, we set up the reserved machine and make it. Different times and expenses are required for different parts, and the different parts are produced at different rates. Consider Machine Number 62 as an example. We keep the jigs there to produce eight different parts. Now, the total utilization of that machine is only about 80 per cent, so the scheduling is quite flexible. But as a production man I am inclined to reduce setup costs by making large lots of each part once I have the machine set up. I realize that this increases our work-in-process inventory. If you could give me some guidelines as to how often to run each part and how much to make each time, I'd be glad to cooperate. Here's a list of the parts we make on Machine 62, their out-of-pocket costs, and so forth" (see Exhibit 15-1 for Langdon's list).

Kyle examined Langdon's information with some care. He knew that no obsolescence was involved with this inventory class, because contracts to supply products to railroads were on a long-term basis. He decided to estimate the carrying costs for this type of inventory (capital costs, storage expense, taxes, and insurance) at 22 per cent per year. He also decided to use a safety stock of fifteen days' usage for each part.

QUESTIONS

1. Calculate the economic order quantity and average inventory in units for each of the eight parts produced on Milling Machine 62 (order quantities and safety stocks must be integers,

but average inventory need not be). Calculate the number of setups per year for each part.

2. Generate a graph of inventory level versus time for Part Number 6210M using the quantities calculated in Question 1.

3. For Part Number 6210M, calculate the yearly total costs of inventory (total of setup and carrying) for the calculated order quantity and safety stock. Compare this cost with the previous yearly total cost, assuming that Langdon kept a fifteen-day safety stock and had previously produced parts twice a year.

4. (At option of the instructor.) In the case, Kyle assumed a safety stock of fifteen days' usage for all eight parts. In real situations, these stocks would represent more or less usage for different parts. Discuss why these differences in safety stock are necessary.

PART III

Capital Budgeting

Graves Specialty Manufacturing

Acceptance/Rejection Decision for an Independent Project (1)

Graves Specialty Manufacturing, a job shop specializing in metal products, had been started in the 1950s and had been fairly successful. The firm operated two production facilities about 100 miles apart, both located in Illinois. Although the firm specialized in fabricating metal items using stamping, machining, and similar metalworking processes, many subassemblies also required plastic parts, so Graves also maintained a small plastics injection molding capacity at both locations. The locations were well situated near industrial centers. This convenience factor, combined with Graves' reputation in the trade for quality work and prompt delivery, had led to substantial patronage, profitability, and growth.

All this did not offset several of Graves' basic problems. Like all job shops, Graves' main line of business was manufacturing small- and medium-sized orders of special items. A customer came in with a blueprint or a sample of the item, for example, a cover plate that might have to be stamped, drilled, and finished. Graves' production people would decide how the item should be produced, then give the customer a price quote based on expected volume. Because each item required a different production process and the number of parts to be produced was generally only a few thousand, it was not economical for Graves to set up a production line, which would mean relocating machines for each order. Thus, like most job shops, the plant layout was by operation; all the stamping machines were in one area, all the lathes in another, and so on. This led to severe problems of inventory flow, control, and storage, because parts were constantly shuffled from operation to operation. These problems were further complicated by the number of different parts and subassemblies that the firm was producing simultaneously, sometimes as many as twenty at each plant.

One of Graves' other problems was a lack of production capacity at one of the plants. The firm's management had considered adding equipment to each of the operations, but that would complicate the inventory flow problem still more.

Mark Yogman, the treasurer of Graves Specialty Manufacturing was aware of these problems and was considering a possible solution: the purchase of a multipurpose programmable machine tool. This tool would increase capacity and could perform several operations that were often done in sequence. The new machine would not contribute much to the inventory flow problem, because that was caused by unfinished parts having to be moved from operation to operation. Because the new machine was semiprogrammable, it would be less expensive than Graves' regular production methods. However, Yogman considered the price tag for the machine quite high at $90,000. In early 1979, he had called a meeting with John Craven, the production supervisor, and Ed Jones, the head of the accounting department.

Craven had liked the idea of the new machine but had some concerns. "Frankly, Mark, I'm rather eager to try this new technology in our shops. If it works out, we might consider replacing some of the machines in our operations with these multipurpose machines as the old ones wear out. However, technology in this area is changing rapidly. Consequently, I'm recommending we estimate the usable life of the machine at a relatively short seven years, and I'm extremely uncertain about the salvage value. Over the period, technology may have advanced so much in machines of this sort that the one we buy today may literally be scrap metal. My guess—and it is strictly that—would be a salvage value of $20,000, allowing for inflation."

Jones had furnished a good deal of information. "I certainly hope that this new machine works out," he said, "because that inventory flow problem is very real. You can't kick your way through either of the plants. I've estimated that once we get the new machine set up and running next year, it will increase earnings after taxes by $10,000 each year. That is, earnings after taxes in each year will be $10,000 higher than if the machine were not purchased. This is based on taking on production jobs similar to those we already have and using a tax rate of 48 per cent. As usual, we will depreciate the machine from the purchase price to the salvage value by the sum-of-years-digits method for tax purposes but by the straight-line method for reporting purposes."

Mark Yogman had wanted to make a decision as soon as possible on the new machine, because it would have to be ordered and paid for immediately so as to be available for use in 1980. In the past, Graves had computed several capital budgeting statistics before making a decision: the payback period (computed using total cash flow), the net present value, and the profitability index. The standard cutoff for the payback period had been three years. Yogman also knew that the firm's cost of capital was about 14 per cent.

QUESTIONS

1. Compute a table of yearly net cash flows associated with the new machine. For purposes of simplicity, you may ignore any applicable investment tax credit.

2. Calculate the payback period, net present value, and profitability index for the new machine. Be sure to justify any discount rates used.

3. Should the firm purchase the new machine? Why or why not?

4. (At the option of the instructor.) For this project, would computing the internal rate of return for the project's cash flows and comparing this to the firm's cost of capital be a valid decision methodology? Why or why not?

Tompkins Mining Company

Acceptance/Rejection Decision for an
Independent Project (2)

Barry Tompkins, a young MBA from West Virginia with an undergraduate degree in mining engineering, had decided to buy a coal mine. He had worked in the coal mining industry for several years and believed he could operate such a business successfully. While at a mine site inspecting some equipment during September 1979, he was approached by Samuel Whitaker, a mine owner, regarding the availability of the Johnson Number 3 mine. Tompkins indicated his interest in purchasing such a mine and over the next few weeks obtained considerable information about the mine that was for sale.

The Johnson Number 3 mine was located in southern West Virginia in the rough mountainous section of the Appalachian highlands. The mine site included about 1,500 acres of land accessible by private road and railroad siding. A lumber company owned the surface and the railroad owned the deep mining rights; these deep mining rights, in turn, were leased on a long-term royalty basis to the Johnson Coal Company. Johnson Number 3 produced a mid-volatile, low-sulphur coal that could be used as a steam coal or a metallurgical coal. It was estimated that the mine property contained approximately 8.5 million tons of potentially recoverable coal, although the recovery of all of this coal was not seen as economical.

Tompkins found that Johnson Coal was asking $2.168 million for the lease, the mine, and the equipment already on the site. The equipment included trailers, temporary wooden buildings,

Exhibit 17-1. TOMPKINS MINING COMPANY

Breakdown of Present and Planned Equipment for Johnson Number 3 Mine Site

Equipment Presently at Site:

Mining equipment (market value to be depreciated over 15 years by the sum-of-years-digits method)	$ 794,306
Cars and trucks (market value to be depreciated over 7 years by the sum-of-years-digits method; new trucks and cars to be purchased at the end of the seventh year at an expected cost of $36,000, and be depreciated over their remaining life of 8 years in the same way)	20,100
Goodwill	1,353,594
Total purchase price	$2,168,000

Equipment to Be Purchased:

(Shown at purchase price; to be depreciated from purchase to end of life in 1994 by the sum-of-years-digits method)	
To be purchased at end of first year	$2,000,000
To be purchased at end of second year	1,800,000
To be purchased at end of third year	1,260,000
Total to be purchased	$5,060,000

mining equipment, autos, trucks, and the cleaning plant. All the equipment was relatively new, having been purchased or constructed over the last three years (a breakdown of the present equipment at Johnson Number 3 is provided in Exhibit 17-1).

Tompkins planned to greatly expand the site's output, which was then about 2,600 tons of coal per month. He intended to cut two additional deep mines on the site, add a second production shift, and make specific changes in supplying the underground crews (a forecast of estimated future site output with these modifications is presented in Exhibit 17-2). To do this, however, would require additional investments totaling $5.06 million over a three-year period for more mining equipment. He had also estimated carefully the direct costs of mining each ton of coal (see Exhibit 17-3). Besides these costs, he knew that he would have to pay a royalty of 8 per cent of the selling price of the coal to the railroad company and a similar royalty of 1.15 per cent of the selling price to the State of West Virginia. The current selling price of coal of the type mined at Johnson

Exhibit 17-2.   TOMPKINS MINING COMPANY

Expected Future Site Output for Johnson
Number 3 Mine Site

Year	Thousands of Tons Output	Year	Thousands of Tons Output
1980	50	1988	220
1981	90	1989	230
1982	105	1990	270
1983	110	1991	300
1984	120	1992	375
1985	160	1993	410
1986	180	1994	480
1987	210		

Number 3, as of late 1979, was about $31 a ton. Tompkins expected this price and his direct costs per ton to rise at about 8 per cent per year after 1980, allowing for a moderate inflation rate, union demands, and an increasing demand for low-sulphur, low-pollution coal. He expected that engineering, accounting, and office expenses would be $30,000 for 1980 and would increase at about 6 per cent per year thereafter; he expected that the useful life of the mine site would be fifteen years. He did not expect to salvage any equipment when the mine's useful life was over. Depletion allowances would accrue to the railroad leasing the land to him. Once the mine was ac-

Exhibit 17-3.   TOMPKINS MINING COMPANY

Expected Direct Costs per Ton of Coal Mined
at Johnson Number 3

Direct mine labor	$ 9.80
Tipple labor	1.60
Social Security	.70
Workman's Compensation	1.40
Black Lung benefits plan	.50
Employee's insurance	.55
Federal Reclamation	.50
Federal Black Lung fund	.15
Safety schooling	.05
Fuels and lubricants	.90
Equipment repairs	.55
Supplies	1.10
Transport	1.15
Total direct costs per ton	$19.15

quired, Tompkins planned to incorporate the venture and expected the effective income tax rate, including state and local income taxes, to be 45 per cent.

QUESTIONS

1. Generate a table of net cash flows associated with the purchase of the mine and the other expenditures that Barry Tompkins had planned.

2. Calculate the net present value of the project. Justify the discount rate that you choose.

3. Calculate the internal rate of return for the project.

4. Should the project be undertaken? Why or why not?

5. (At option of the instructor.) It is often said that the net present value method assigns higher risk premiums to later flows. Why is this true? Is this a serious problem in using the net present value evaluation method for this case? Why or why not?

Webster's Lumberyard

Replacement Analysis

No one could say that John Webster's lumber distribution business had not been successful. Since he had started the firm ten years ago, profits had been substantial and the firm had grown to three locations in adjacent cities. In late 1979, Webster was considering the purchase of a small-business computer system to support the firm's expanding volume.

The use of minicomputers for small businesses was an outgrowth of the development of integrated electronic circuits, or "chips." These circuits, originally developed for application in the U.S. space program, combined the functions of several electronic components (semiconductors, resistors, and others) into one microscopic unit. The mass production of such chips had lowered tremendously the cost of logic circuitry, making possible computers that small businesses could afford (inexpensive hand-held calculators were also an outgrowth of this effect). The development of inexpensive data-storage devices, such as the "floppy disk," had made computers practical for firms of the size of Webster's Lumberyard or even smaller.

The acquisition of a minicomputer system had been suggested by the firm's accountant, Ms. Harvey, who pointed out that such a system could also be used for inventory control, a major problem for the firm. Ms. Harvey, who had been with the firm on a full-time basis for about two years, believed that she could handle the operation of the computer on a day-to-day basis; she had taken computer programming courses in college.

None of these courses, however, had been in the languages used by the minicomputer systems that were being considered; consequently, she and Webster agreed that the basic software (programs) for any system would be purchased rather than developed by Ms. Harvey. This also would reduce the time necessary to get the system "on line." On the basis of some discussion with a friend of Ms..Harvey, who had some experience with minicomputers, Webster and Ms. Harvey decided that the minimum computing power necessary for the functions they had in mind would be satisfied by two systems that were then on the market: the RAM-ROM 85 and the KD-126. These sys-

Exhibit 18-1. WEBSTER'S LUMBERYARD

Bids on RAM-ROM 85 and KD-126 Computer Systems

RAM-ROM 85 System
Main Memory Capacity: 32K Words MOS Random Access
Power Consumption When Operating: 650 Watts for
Units Described as Follows:

Hardware:	
RAM-ROM 85 computer & video terminal, expansion interface, 2 floppy disk drives, hard-copy printer, system desk	$4,191.00
Software:	
Computer language course	29.95
General ledger program	99.95
Payroll program	199.95
Inventory program	199.95

Software has been produced by a team of the manufacturer's professional programmers.

KD-126 System
Main Memory Capacity: 16K Words MOS
Random Access
Power Consumption When Operating: 820 Watts
for Units Described as Follows:

Hardware:	
KD-126 computer	$1,895.00
Video terminal	995.00
2 floppy disk drives	2,595.00
Hard-copy printer	895.00
Memory expansion module to 32K words	480.00
Interface	100.00
System desk	295.00
Software:	
Computer language course	39.95

tems, sold by two different companies, used slightly different computer languages. Webster asked the two computer manufacturers to submit bids on a system adequate for his needs. These bids are reproduced in Exhibit 18-1.

As soon as the bids were received, Webster put in a call to the manufacturer of the KD-126 system. He had asked for quotes on general accounting, payroll, and inventory management software, he had said, and inquired as to why these had not been included. The manufacturer replied that the firm did not provide software in this way, but instead kept a library of user-submitted programs that would undoubtedly contain what Webster wanted; copies of these programs were submitted free of charge to KD-126 purchasers. This did not please Webster very much, because he would have preferred a more formal and businesslike approach to the software area, but he also believed that the KD-126 computer system was probably technically superior (from an electronic sense) to the RAM-ROM 85 system. He turned over the quotes to Ms. Harvey for evaluation.

In deciding between the systems, Ms. Harvey decided to assume a relatively short life of five years. She also decided to assume that the system would be used three and a half hours per work day during the first year and that this usage would increase by one half hour a day during each successive year; the firm's electricity cost was four cents per kilowatt hour. She decided that the firm would probably have to spend about $200 per year on incidental additional expenses such as paper for the hard-copy printer.

QUESTIONS

1. Generate a table of net cash flows for each of the two alternatives, assuming a $1,500 salvage value for either system. Use the sum-of-years-digits depreciation method and a 15 per cent discount rate. State all other assumptions.

2. Calculate the net present value of each of the two alternative systems.

3. Discuss some nonquantitative factors that should be taken into consideration in deciding between the two alternatives.

4. Which alternative should be chosen? Why?

5. (At option of the instructor.) Is internal rate of return a useful capital budgeting procedure in replacement analysis? Why or why not?

MIY Enterprises Corporation

Abandonment Analysis

MIY Enterprises was a chemical firm with plants located at seven sites throughout the United States. One of the firm's products was a rubberlike plastic sold under the trade name "Resilient." The firm made the plastic in a relatively new facility at its extensive West Virginia plant site. The facility had been built in the early 1970s, but because of technical problems in producing batches of the material of consistent quality and properties, sales had been quite disappointing. (See Exhibit 19-1 for the fiscal 1975 income statement for the Resilient unit of MIY Enterprises.) Sales were expected to increase only marginally in the upcoming years, and the firm frankly considered the entire Resilient venture to be a "flop." As a result, in early 1976 the management considered abandoning the product line and selling the associated marketing knowledge, copyrights, patents, and plant machinery to a competitor. The competitor had recently made a firm offer of $5 million (adjusted for taxes). To evaluate whether the offer should be accepted, MIY Enterprises decided to use a capital budgeting technique called "abandonment analysis."[1] In this analysis, the present value of abandoning a project at some future time is compared with the value of immediate abandonment. If any present value

---

[1] See A. A. Robicheck and J. C. Van Horne, "Abandonment Value and Capital Budgeting," *Journal of Finance*, December, 1967, pp. 557-89.

Exhibit 19-1. MIY ENTERPRISES CORPORATION

Income Statement for Tax Purposes of Resilient
Unit for Fiscal 1975

Sales	$14,176,000
Direct materials	11,341,000
Direct labor	2,126,000
Depreciation	2,400,000
Earnings before tax	(1,691,000)
Tax savings	778,000
Earnings after tax	$ (913,000)

Note: ROI based on year-end investment book
value of $6 million: (15.2) per cent

of the future abandonment is greater than the value of immediate abandonment, the project is not immediately abandoned.[2]

The analysis procedure is as follows:

1. Compute the net present value of the project for its maximum usable life.

2. Compare this net present value with the value of immediate abandonment. If it is greater than immediate abandonment value, do not abandon immediately, reevaluate the project at a later date.

3. If the net present value of the project based on its maximum usable life is less than that of immediate abandonment, the present value of alternatives of abandoning the projects at various future times must be evaluated. These are computed one at a time, starting with one fiscal period before the maximum usable life, followed by two periods before the maximum usable life, and so on. After a present value of abandoning at a future time is computed, it is compared with the value of immediate abandonment. The process stops when either: (a) a present value of abandonment at some future time is greater than the value of immediate abandonment, or (b) all future periods of possible abandonment are exhausted. In the first instance, the project is not immediately abandoned but is reviewed at a later time. In the second, no present value of future abandonment is greater than the value of immediate abandonment, so the project is abandoned immediately.

Exhibit 19-2 presents the abandonment analysis methodology

[2] Note that firms should probably perform such an analysis for all their projects during each financial period so that projects could be discontinued when funds could be better utilized elsewhere.

Exhibit 19-2. MIY ENTERPRISES CORPORATION

Flowchart of Abandonment Analysis Procedure,
Using Yearly Cash Flows and Yearly Reviews

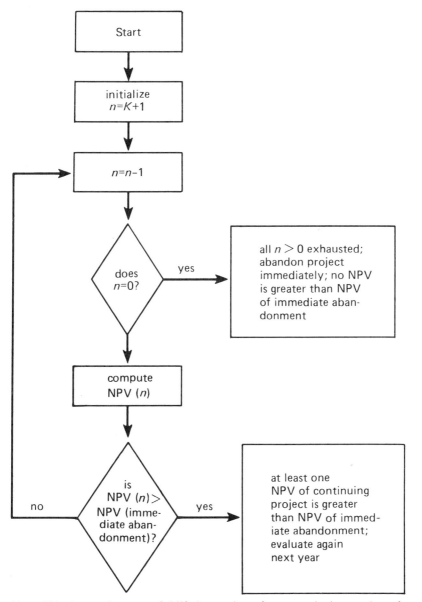

Here, K is the maximum useful life in number of years; n is the number of years of operation for which the net present value is being computed. For example, if a project has a maximum usable life of 3 years, the $n=3$ condition means "hold for maximum life then abandon" and the $n=2$ condition means "hold for two years, then abandon."

Exhibit 19–3. MIY ENTERPRISES CORPORATION

Projected Partial Income Statements for Tax Purposes and Abandonment Values for Resilient Unit

Fiscal Year	1976	1977	1978	1979	1980	1981	1982	1983
Sales (thou.)	$14,389	$14,604	$14,824	$15,046	$15,272	$15,501	$15,733	$15,969
Costs* (thou.)	15,670	15,474	15,283	15,094	14,908	14,726	14,946	15,171
Abandonment cash flow unit at end of fiscal year, including tax adjustments (thou.)	4,000	3,670	3,330	3,000	2,670	2,330	2,000	2,000

*Includes direct materials, direct labor, and depreciation.

in flowchart form on the basis of yearly evaluation and yearly cash flow periods.

The planners at MIY Enterprises had determined that the equipment used in making Resilient had a useful economic life of eight years at a maximum. It was, however, being depreciated to a zero salvage over five years by the sum-of-year-digits method for tax purposes. In early 1976 the equipment had a book value of $6 million (the original life was nine years and the original book value, $18 million). Partial projected income statements and abandonment values are presented in Exhibit 19-3. These estimated abandonment values declined in the early years (1976 through 1982) because of the wearing-out and consequent decline in resale value of the equipment. However, these abandonment value estimates also included a $2 million price for the land on which the Resilient production facility rested. The firm's other operations at its West Virginia site were expected to need expansion, and the alternative to using the Resilient area was the purchase of additional land. Thus, included in the estimated abandonment cash flows, along with the equipment salvage, was an opportunity cost of not having to purchase such land. This opportunity cost was not expected to decline over time.

QUESTIONS

1. Generate a table of yearly projected net cash flows from operations of the Resilient product line for each of the years 1976 to 1983. Flows of this sort will occur, of course, only if operations of the product line are continued in each of the corresponding years.

2. Execute the abandonment analysis algorithm for the Resilient product line. You may use a 12 per cent discount rate. Decide whether the line should be sold to the competitor; justify your decision. (*Note:* As of early 1975, MIY Enterprises also had the option of immediately scrapping the Resilient product line, but the present value of this option was somewhat lower than the competitor's offer, so that the immediate scrapping option was rejected out of hand. Thus, the immediate abandonment value is the competitor's purchase offer in this case.)

3. (At option of the instructor.) In the case, the Resilient product line and its associated assets were a very small part of the firm's overall sales and asset picture. Suppose the product

line under consideration were much larger, say 20 per cent of the firm's sales and assets (in the early 1980s many firms sold off divisions or units of such a size). Discuss the effect abandonment would then have on the firm's business risk and its cost of capital.

Jones Supply, Inc.

Assessing Risk, Using Coefficients of Variation

Jones Supply, Inc. was a small manufacturer of industrial products located in eastern Florida. In late 1979, James Steele, the firm's financial officer, received a request from Samuel Elkins, the firm's production manager, to review the alternatives for the purchase of a new production machine for the firm. An old turret lathe had worn out and had to be replaced. The alternatives had been narrowed to two on the basis of technical considerations: a manual-style lathe similar to the one that had worn out, and a partially automatic machine. The second machine did not cost much more than the first but was expected to reduce after-tax costs, in comparison to not replacing the worn-out machine at all, by a considerably larger amount. On reviewing the expected cash flows, Steele telephoned Elkins.

"Sam, I can't see where there is any debate here between the two machines," he said. "If either is a good idea, it must be the newer-style machine according to these expected cash flows. Why didn't you eliminate the old-style machine initially?"

"It isn't all that clear to me that the newer-style machine is all that much better, Jim," Elkins replied. "There are other considerations. It is true that the partially automatic machine has a faster production rate and thus lowers costs more on long production runs. However, it takes longer to set up and therefore has higher costs on shorter runs. If we get a deep recession and order sizes from our customers are reduced, the cost savings from the newer style machine will drop faster. On the other

Exhibit 20-1. JONES SUPPLY, INC.

Increases in After-Tax Earnings Associated with the Purchase
of Alternative Turret Lathes

Old-Style Machine (Initial Investment: $10,000)

Yr.	EAT Increase if Economic Conditions are Worse than Expected	EAT Increase if Economic Conditions are as Expected	EAT Increase if Economic Conditions are Better than Expected
1	$ 1,500	$2,000	$2,500
2	1,250	1,750	2,250
3	1,000	1,500	2,000
4	750	1,250	1,750
5	500	1,000	1,500
6	250	750	1,250
7	0	500	1,000

New-Style Machine (Initial Investment: $17,500)

1	$ 2,000	$4,000	$6,000
2	1,500	3,500	5,500
3	1,000	3,000	5,000
4	500	2,500	4,500
5	0	2,000	4,000
6	-500	1,500	3,500
7	-1,000	1,000	3,000

hand, if we get a boom period, they will rise faster. I'll set up
some more data for you on both machines. You tell me what
your financial analysis says."

Steele received the additional data from Elkins a few days
later (see Exhibit 20-1). These estimates were based on the
expected state of the economy. In late 1979, it was expected
that the country was about to go into a recession, followed by
a recovery at some future period. As in all economic forecasts,
however, there was some degree of uncertainty attached to
these expectations, but the near term was probably more certain than forecasts further in the future. Elkins therefore decided to incorporate these increasing uncertainties into his
methodology by changing his probabilities over time (see
Exhibit 20-2). He knew that both machine alternatives had the
same expected life, seven years, and that both were to be depreciated to a zero salvage by the sum-of-years-digits method.
Following the logic of risk-adjusted discount rates, he wanted to
compare the two machines by assigning a higher discount rate

Exhibit 20-2. JONES SUPPLY, INC.

Probabilities of Various Economic Conditions As Estimated by Mr. Steele

Yr.	Probability that Economic Conditions will be Worse than Expected	Probability that Economic Conditions will be About as Expected	Probability that Economic Conditions will be Better than Expected
1	.150	.700	.150
2	.175	.650	.175
3	.200	.600	.200
4	.225	.550	.225
5	.250	.500	.250
6	.275	.450	.275
7	.300	.400	.300

to the more risky alternative. He knew that the firm's marginal cost of capital was 10 per cent.

QUESTIONS

1. Compute the coefficients of variation of the net cash flows in each period of each alternative machine. Which is more risky? Does this risk increase or decrease over time? Why or why not?

2. Compute the expected net present values of the two alternatives. Justify the discount rate or rates used.

3. Which alternative should be selected? Why?

4. (At option of the instructor.) If the errors in the economic forecasts are assumed to be independent, the two alternatives can be examined in another way: by calculating the expected net present value and the standard deviation of net present value and examining these for the two alternatives. The risk-free, after-tax rate of interest is usually used as a discount rate in such calculations; you may assume that this is 5 per cent. Calculate the expected net present value and the standard deviation of the net present value for the two alternatives under these assumptions. Use the following formula:

$$\text{standard deviation of NPV} = \left(\sum_{t=1}^{n} \frac{SD(NCF_t)^2}{(1+k)^{2t}} \right)^{\frac{1}{2}}$$

Where n is the project life, $SD(NCF_t)^2$ is the variance of the net cash flow in period t, and k is the discount rate. How would Steele make a decision using these calculated values?

Consumer Products, Inc.

Decision Trees

Consumer Products, Inc. was a small, regional producer of small appliances and household goods such as garbage cans, plastic pitchers, and other similar products. In early 1979, the firm's management decided to produce a new product that would have several uses: a rack for standard-sized baby food jars. The rack was about one foot high and wide and three inches deep, and initial versions were fabricated of metal and plastic. The rack could hold a dozen jars and was intended to be mounted flat against a wall or inside a kitchen cabinet. Besides the obvious use as a space-saver and organizer for baby food containers in the kitchen, the rack also had uses in the workshop. Once baby food jars were empty, the firm knew that it was common for families to clean them out and use them to organize and store small nails, screws, bolts, and the like. The rack could also be used to hold jars for these uses. Also, because the rack was to be priced at only $2.49 at retail, using baby food jars and the rack to hold small parts was cheaper than buying a small parts cabinet, which usually sold for about $4.00.

One problem had been apparent early in planning to produce the rack, however. The firm had no surplus capacity at its plant available for manufacture of the product. Consequently, some capital investment would be necessary for new plastic molding and metal working equipment. How much investment would be necessary depended on how many production lines the firm planned to set up. Because Consumer Products, Inc. was not financially very sophisticated, it was decided to consult with John Preston, who was on the staff of a local college, regarding the capital investment decision.

In talking with the executives of Consumer Products, Preston found that the firm was considering a number of courses of action. Because demand for the new product was uncertain, one initial option was to start with one production line to determine what demand existed for the product. The executive of the firm in charge of marketing and sales, Jack Nelson, decided for purposes of analysis to estimate the demand for the output of the first production line in terms of two levels: high demand and low demand. Nelson had assessed the probabilities of these two levels as 0.6 and 0.4, respectively. Nelson believed it would take three years to determine the demand level. At that time the firm could decide whether to expand to a second production line or to stay with one line. The level of demand that occurred for the first line would, of course, give some information on demand for the second line. Nelson estimated that if the firm experienced high demand for the output of the first line, the probabilities of high demand and low demand for the output of

Exhibit 21-1. CONSUMER PRODUCTS, INC.

Project Cash Flow Forecast in Rounded Thousands of Dollars

Condition	Year							
	0	1	2	3	4	5	6	7
One line throughout								
High demand	−100	40	50	40	30	20	10	5
Low demand	−100	20	35	20	20	10	5	5
Start with one line, go to two in third year								
High demand for both lines	−100	40	50	−70	60	40	20	10
Low demand for both lines	−100	20	35	−90	40	20	10	10
High demand for first line, low for second line	−100	40	50	−70	50	30	15	10
Low demand for first line, high for second line	−100	20	35	−90	50	30	15	10
Two lines throughout								
High demand	−200	80	100	80	60	40	20	10
Low demand	−200	40	70	40	40	20	10	10

the second line would be 0.9 and 0.1, respectively. If the firm experienced low demand for the output of the first line, on the other hand, Nelson estimated that the probabilities of high and low demand for the output of the second line would be 0.2 and 0.8, respectively. However, the firm would have to "pay" for this information because the installation of the two lines at different times would cost considerably more than if both lines were installed initially. Installation of the first line would cost $100,000, and installation of the second three years later would cost $110,000. If, however, the firm elected to install both lines immediately, the total installation cost would be $200,000. Nelson estimated the probabilities of high and low demand for the output of the two lines, if both were installed initially, at 0.5 and 0.5, respectively.

On the basis of certain marketing conditions, Preston elected to use seven years as the life of the project. His estimates of cash flows for various decisions and demand levels are presented in Exhibit 21-1; the installation costs of the lines are included in these cash flow estimates. Preston decided on 10 per cent as an appropriate discount rate.

QUESTIONS

1. Compute the net present values for the various decisions and outcomes shown in Exhibit 21-1.

2. Because the capital budgeting problem here involves sequential decisions over time, the appropriate method of analysis is a decision tree. Draw the decision tree for the case, post the net present values in the appropriate locations, and perform the necessary rollback procedure.

3. What should Preston recommend that Consumer Products, Inc. do? Why?

4. (At option of the instructor.) In decision tree analysis net present values are usually used as the capital budgeting decision criteria. It would also be possible to use internal rate of return; however, many decision tree situations involve additional expenditures after the initial period. This can cause a problem in using internal rate of return. Discuss this problem, using as an example the "start with one line, go to two lines in the third year, high demand for both lines" condition.

Westmoreland Estates

Capital Budgeting for Real Estate (1)*

Westmoreland Estates was a real estate development made up of five twelve-unit apartment buildings. Three of these buildings were two-bedroom units, and the remaining two buildings housed one-bedroom units. All were brick buildings with redwood decks. The complex was located at 2950 Auburn Road, Huntington, West Virginia. The property was composed of two separate lots, which are legally described in Exhibit 22-1. Exhibits 22-2 and 22-3 provide details of the lots and locations of the buildings.

Huntington, West Virginia is located to the southwest of the geographic center of the state and on the Ohio River. It lies fifty-five miles to the west of the state's capital, Charleston. It borders on Ohio and Kentucky.

Major highways serving Huntington are U.S. Routes 60 and Interstate 64, both passing East-West through the city. Conveniently accessible are state Routes 75 and 52, which pass North-South adjacent to Huntington.

Tri-State Airport, West Virginia's second largest transportation facility, in Huntington, offers commercial jet service to all major Eastern cities. The Norfolk and Western and the Chesapeake and Ohio Railroads provide industrial rail service, and Amtrak passenger service is available.

*This case was contributed by Ms. Lee Ann Ferguson and Dr. George Moody. It is designed for educational purposes and not for research or to illustrate the correct or incorrect handling of administrative practices.

Exhibit 22-1. WESTMORELAND ESTATES

Legal Description of Land Parcels

Parcel No. 1. Beginning at a stake in the north line of the paved road, 172 feet easterly from the line of the property formerly known as the E. W. Forgery land; thence with the northerly line of said paved road N. 69° 33' E. 140 feet to a stake; thence leaving said paved road N. 20° 27' W. 477.44 feet to a stake; thence S. 36° 15' W. 107.37 feet to a stake; thence S. 20° 27' E. 477.44 feet to the north side of said paved road; thence E. 10° 107.37 feet to the point of beginning, containing 1.67 acres, more or less, EXCEPTING and RESERVING, however, a portion of the above-described property together with permanent easement and right of way, conveyed to the City of Huntington, a municipal corporation, by Condemnation Order of the Circuit Court of Wayne County, West Virginia, entered in the records of said court on March 10, 1941.

Parcel No. 2. Beginning at a point in the north line of Auburn Road, which point is easterly with said line, 72 feet from the southwest corner of the Mariah E. Circle lot, said beginning point being also easterly 63 feet from the point of intersection of the said north line of Auburn Road with the west line of Camden Road, produced; thence northerly at right angles to the said line of Auburn Road, 477.44 feet to a point in the flood wall south right of way line; thence with said line, westerly 135.52 feet; thence leaving the said right of way line, southerly at right angles to the said line of Auburn Road, 428.24 feet and then easterly to the point of BEGINNING.

The trading area has a combined population of 571,000. The population of the metropolitan area, where the largest manufacturing employers are metalworking firms, producers of transportation equipment, and producers of glass products, is 286,935. Some 105,700 people are employed in the metropolitan area. The unemployment rate stood at 7.4 per cent in 1980. Employment in the area was diversified, with 26,800 people engaged in manufacturing and the balance in nonmanufacturing occupations. The principal employers in the area were Huntington Alloys, employing 2,900; ACF Industries, employing 1,651; Owens-Illinois, employing 1,416; and Conners Steel, employing 1,063. All other employers had less than 1,000 employees.

Although industry is the main source of employment in the area, state and city workers were employed at the area's four large hospitals, the local university, and several small colleges. Construction activity had remained relatively steady, with slight dropoffs during periods of exceptionally high interest rates, and real estate had been selling close to list price, given an adequate selling period.

Good schools were available at the elementary, junior-high, and high school levels. The town had a city manager form of

Exhibit 22-2. WESTMORELAND ESTATES

Plot Locations

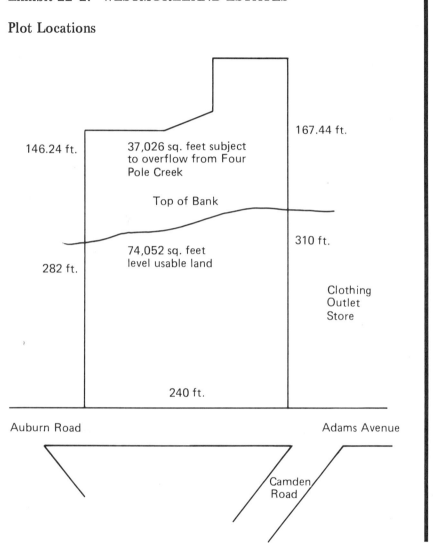

government, and police, fire, and emergency ambulance departments. Most of the retail trade stores were located in downtown Huntington, but some retail stores were dispersed throughout the city and in a new mall on the outskirts.

Westmoreland Estates lay in an area on the north side of Auburn Road; east of the site was an area used for retail business. West of the site, Auburn Road was almost completely developed with single-family, owner-occupied homes in the $40,000 price range. South of the site, along Camden Road,

Exhibit 22-3. WESTMORELAND ESTATES

Approximate Building Locations

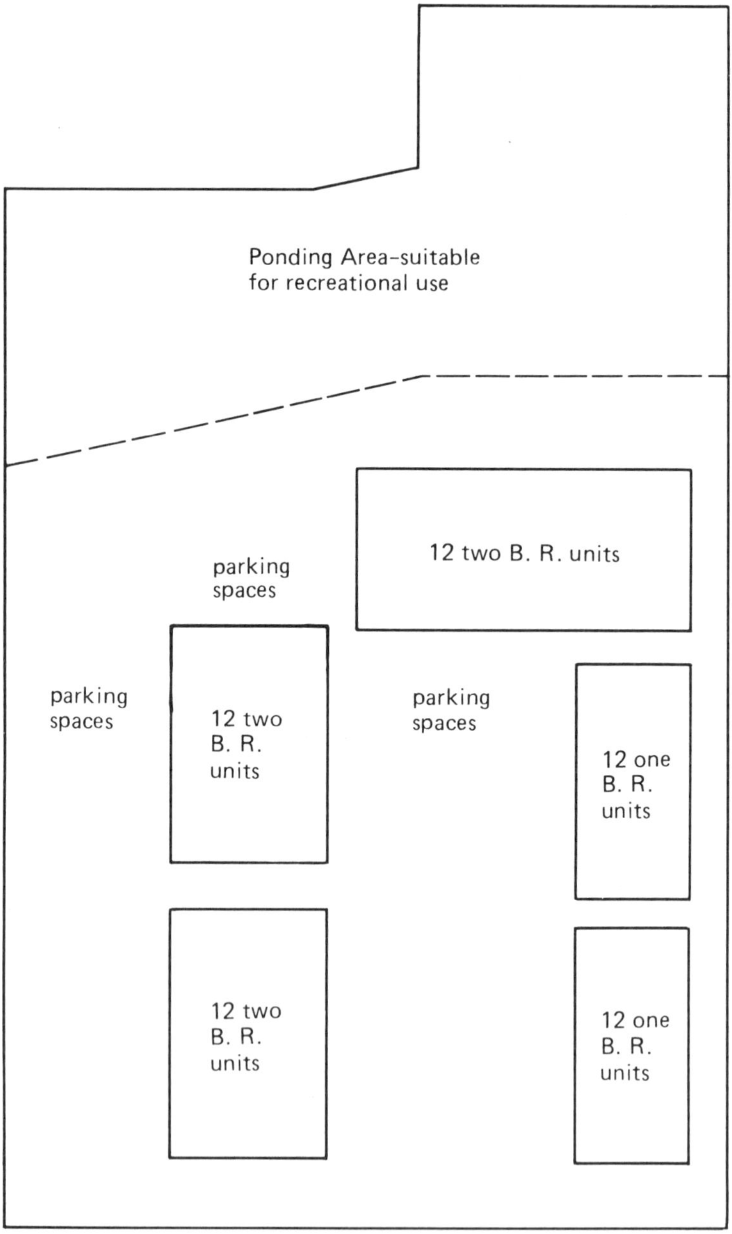

Ponding Area-suitable
for recreational use

12 two B. R. units

parking
spaces

parking
spaces

12 two
B. R.
units

parking
spaces

12 one
B. R.
units

12 two
B. R.
units

12 one
B. R.
units

land use was retail, with a neighborhood shopping center about one half block from the complex. The neighborhood was served by public transportation. The area was classified as a residential area with a very limited transition to local business. The complex was within walking distance of schools, grocers, and several local businesses.

Exhibit 22-4. WESTMORELAND ESTATES

Rents for Similar Complexes in Huntington

Greentree Apartments, 3555 Route 60, East, Huntington, West Virginia
    1-bedroom units—$325.00/mo.
    2-bedroom units—$385.00/mo.

Country Club Apartments, Country Club Drive, Route 60, Huntington
    1-bedroom units—$310.00/mo.
    2-bedroom units—$375.00/mo.

Westchester Apartments, 2950 5th Avenue, Huntington
    1-bedroom units—$315.00/mo.
    2-bedroom units—$375.00/mo.

Lynwood Apartments, 6th Avenue, Huntington
    2-bedroom units—$285.00/mo.

Greenbrier Gardens, 924 10th Avenue, Huntington
    2-bedroom units—$385.00/mo.

Several other complexes in the Huntington area were similar to Westmoreland Estates. A list of these complexes and their rental charges at the time of the case are in Exhibit 22-4. As shown, the monthly rents of $280 for a one-bedroom unit and $360 for a two-bedroom unit, the rents in effect at Westmoreland Estates at the time of the case, were in line with, if not below, rents charged in similar facilities. Considering the relative newness of Westmoreland Estates, and the availability of laundries and parking spaces, it was expected that rents for the units would hold at this level through 1982 and then be increased at a rate of 4 per cent per year. Apartment plans for the one- and two-bedroom units are presented in Exhibit 22-5.

The complex was completed in 1980. The land was purchased for $120,000 and was equity-financed. The buildings cost $1.4 million, debt-financed using a 12 per cent, twenty-year mortgage. Monthly payments on this mortgage were $14,745.14.

Depreciation on this apartment complex for tax purposes was computed by the straight-line method with an estimated life of

Exhibit 22-5. WESTMORELAND ESTATES

Typical Floor Plans of Rental Units

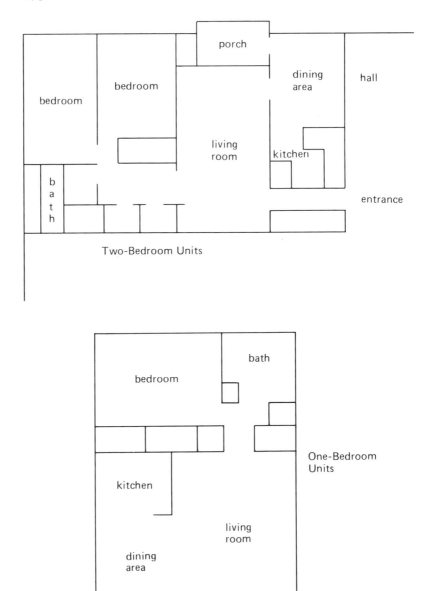

thirty years. Thus, yearly depreciation on the $1.4 million investment in the buildings was $46,667.

The problem faced by Ms. Lee Ann Ferguson, a relative of the development's owner, in late 1981 was to estimate a value for the property and a rate of return on her family's currently invested capital. In this way, purchase offers for the development and alternative investment opportunities could be evaluated. She decided to assume the following:

1. The development would be kept for ten years, then sold for $2.1 million.

2. The vacancy rate would be 3 per cent.

3. Total operating expenses (water, cable television, and so on) would be 15 per cent of annual rental income, net of vacancy expense.

4. Real estate taxes would be 10 per cent of net rental income.

5. There would be a 50 per cent tax on regular income and a 20 per cent tax on capital gains.

QUESTIONS

1. Generate a table of yearly cash flows for the Westmoreland Estates complex for the next ten years including cash flows from the sale of the complex. You may assume that the analysis is taking place early in 1982; the cash flows will then be for the years 1982 through 1991.

2. Calculate the net present value of the development as of early 1982. Justify the discount rate chosen based on the financing package involved, the risk of the project, and the family's likely required rate of return on equity.

3. Calculate the internal rate of return on the project assuming an initial, early 1982 cost of $1.52 million.

4. (At option of the instructor.) One major difference between capital budgeting in real estate and in other areas of business is the connection between the financing package and the evaluated assets. In the usual non-real-estate analysis, the project is evaluated independently of the arrangements used to finance it. Discuss how this differs in real estate evaluations when mortgages are assumable.

Block Fifty-Two

Capital Budgeting for Real Estate (2)

In late 1981, Martin Lawrence was considering the purchase of some income-producing property in Greatankle, New Jersey. Greatankle was a commuting area for New York City; Lawrence lived in Greatankle and made the commute daily. Lawrence was a relatively successful businessman, taxed at 50 per cent on marginal ordinary income, and was looking for an investment that would yield some income sheltering through depreciation. When Block 52, lots 49, 50, 51, and 51A came up for sale in Greatankle, he decided to investigate this investment opportunity (see Exhibit 23-1 for a plot plan of this property).

The asking price for the property was $320,000, but Lawrence knew that the final selling price would be lower, probably around $300,000, net of selling costs. The property consisted of three buildings and a gravel parking lot. The first building was a 40 × 45 -foot real estate office. Next to this was a 70 × 55 -foot building, formerly the town post office, but now housing a well-established liquor store. The last building was by far the largest, a two-story building with exterior first-story dimensions of 95 × 75-feet. Four income-producing units were incorporated in this building: three first-floor storefronts and a second-floor apartment. The storefronts were occupied by a law office, a delicatessen, and a candy store. All three businesses had been at that location a minimum of three years; the candy store, a landmark in downtown Greatankle, had been at the location for more than thirty years.

Exhibit 23-1. BLOCK FIFTY-TWO

Plot Plan of Involved Properties

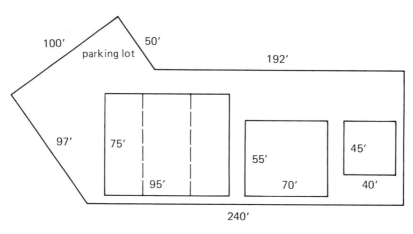

Lawrence knew that the ability of income property to consistently generate revenues depended on the financial health of the surrounding community. Here trends seemed very favorable. Greatankle and the surrounding county had benefited from the migration of firms' headquarters away from downtown Manhattan and into New Jersey, Connecticut, and other parts of New York State. During the 1970s, several firms had moved to Greatankle or adjoining towns (Greatankle was relatively small, with a population of only 9,000). The town had good public transportation with a local bus line and a train to New York City. The Garden State Parkway, a major highway in New Jersey, was near the town also. Good public and private schools were available, as were recreational facilities, including a public library, three parks, two private swim clubs, and a roller skating rink.

Upon investigation of the property and consideration of his personal situation, Lawrence was able to make several estimates. First, because of his retirement plans, he assumed that he would sell the property after ten years. Over this period, he expected property values in the Greatankle area to increase by 8 per cent per year. Any capital gain on the sale of the property would, of course, be taxed at the capital gains rate, which at the time was 40 per cent of the seller's regular tax rate. Selling costs, he expected, would total 10 per cent of sale price when he sold the property. For 1981, the six total income-producing units rented for $39,700 and had total expenses of $14,687. Lawrence decided to assume a 5 per cent rate for yearly rent increases and expense increases. Although there had been no vacancies in 1981, he also decided to use a 5 per cent vacancy rate in future years. He was advised by his tax accountant that he could use the 125 per cent declining balance method for depreciation on the buildings and a 15-year life; of the $300,000 estimated sale price, buildings would comprise $240,000 and land, $60,000. Lawrence expected to finance the project by investing $75,000 in savings and using a 17.5 per cent, 25-year mortgage for the remaining $225,000.

QUESTIONS

1. Generate a table of projected net cash flows for the property over Lawrence's expected holding period.

2. Calculate the internal rate of return for the purchase of Block 52.

3. Indicate whether Block 52 constitutes an acceptable project for Lawrence. Include in your response the identification of sources of risk for the project. (*Note:* As of late 1981, good-grade corporate bonds were yielding about 14 per cent interest).

4. (At option of the instructor.) All capital projects have some degree of risk. Indicate how Lawrence could assess the degree of risk in the Block 52 investment project had he access to a small computer. What outputs would be involved? How would these be used?

Thackers Run Watershed

*Capital Budgeting in the Public Sector**

Thackers Run Watershed, located in southwestern West Virginia, has an area of 36,733 acres, or 57.4 square miles. It is a rural area of scattered farms, small communities, and one town. In 1978 an estimated 3,197 people resided in the watershed, of which 1,397 lived in Maidsville, the only incorporated town.

The major problems of the watershed are frequent flooding of residences, agricultural land, businesses, industry, roads, bridges, and utilities. It is anticipated that an additional source of municipal water will be needed because of the considerable growth anticipated in or adjacent to Maidsville as a result of new deep mine openings in the area.

The local people are considering certain structural measures to alleviate these problems. The proposed measures consist of a multiple-purpose site for floodwater control and water supply purposes and 2.5 miles of flood prevention channel work. Technical assistance is being provided by the Soil Conservation Service.

The goals of the local people are to (1) provide flood damage protection in the urban area from a 100-year-frequency storm, (2) provide a five-year level of protection in agricultural areas, and (3) develop additional municipal and industrial water supplies for Maidsville, West Virginia.

*Contributed by Dr. William Riley, West Virginia University.

Construction cost estimates for the multipurpose structure were made at current prices. Unit prices were obtained from bids for work of similar nature and were adjusted for location and topography. A contingency allowance of 12 per cent was added to the final estimate to allow for solving any unusual construction problems. The estimated construction cost of the multipurpose structure is $380,300. An additional cost of $30,400 was estimated for engineering services, which include expenditures for surveys, investigations, design and preparation of plans, and construction specifications. Land rights cost is estimated at $565,000. This sum includes the replacement and relocation of roads, gas lines, gas wells, power lines, the purchase of land and buildings, and contingency for anticipated legal fees and surveys. Costs were based on estimates made by qualified appraisers, local people, utility companies, and the State Department of Highways. An additional cost of $25,000 was estimated for relocation payments to homeowners.

The estimated construction cost of 2.5 miles of channel work is $1,005,500. Some of the significant cost items included in this figure are $369,000 for concrete, $58,000 for rock riprap, $359,000 for excavation, and $34,000 for vegetation. In addition, $40,200 was estimated for engineering services and $25,700 for land rights.

Project administration costs include contract administration, relocation assistance advisory services, administrative functions connected with relocation payments, review of engineering plans, and necessary inspection service during construction to ensure that structural measures are installed in accordance with the plans and specifications. The total estimated cost of project administration is $172,300.

For a breakdown of when the various construction, engineering services, land rights, relocation payments, and project administration costs will be incurred, see Exhibit 24-1.

In addition to the costs associated with construction of the multipurpose structure and channel, operation, maintenance, and replacement cost includes an estimated annual expenditure of $1,200 for the multipurpose structure and $9,900 for the channel works. These costs will be incurred throughout the 100-year project life. Included are such items as repair of concrete work; removal of debris and sediment deposits from the channel area; repair, shaping, and seeding of channel banks; replacement of worn-out elements of the structure; repair of eroded areas in the vicinity of the dam and spillway; and maintenance of water inlet and outlet. The design life of the multipurpose structure and channel is 100 years; however,

Exhibit 24-1. THACKERS RUN WATERSHED

Estimated Costs During Installation Period

Year	Project	Const.*	Engr. Servc.	Project Admin.	Purch. of Land & Bld.	Utility Relocate	Road Relocate*	Legal Fees & Surveys	Relo-cation Payment	Total Initial Ex-penditures
1	Multipurpose Structure		$30,400		$54,800	$75,200		$1,800		$162,200
2	Multipurpose Structure	$143,988		$33,400			$192,278		$25,000	394,666
3	Multipurpose Structure	191,132		33,300			189,458			413,890
4	Channel		40,200		21,000	3,700		1,000		65,900
5	Channel	443,067		52,800						495,867
6	Channel	442,979		52,800						495,779

*Net of savings from employment of now unemployed workers.

115

Exhibit 24-2. THACKERS RUN WATESHED

Estimated Average Annual Flood Damage (With and
Without the Project)

Item	Without Project	With Project
Floodwater		
Residential	$ 7,800	$ 0
Commercial and industrial	21,100	200
Transportation and utilities	23,900	800
Crop and pasture	5,200	3,200
Other agricultural	6,200	300
Municipal water supply	3,100	1,900
Indirect	16,000	3,900
Total average annual damage	$83,300	$10,300

future usefulness of the dam and channel may continue beyond this time period.

A 100-year-frequency flood can be expected to inundate approximately 1,046 acres of land. The current value of the property subject to flooding is estimated at $12 million. Total expected direct and indirect flood damages amount to $83,300 annually (see Exhibit 24-2). The proposed project will provide flood damage protection in the urban area from a 100-year-frequency storm. The annual direct and indirect flood damages with the proposed structural measures are estimated to be $10,300. These floodwater reduction benefits are attributable to either the multipurpose structure or the channel (see Exhibit 24-3) and will begin accruing immediately after each project measure is installed. A portion of the benefits will begin accruing to property adjacent to the channel as soon as the corresponding segment of the channel is completed. Direct floodwater damages include all reduction in physical damages, and indirect floodwater damages include those incurred as a result of direct damages. An example is spoiled food in a supermarket located outside the area flooded but caused by downed power lines in the flood area.

Water supply benefits are considered equivalent to the least expensive alternative for providing municipal and industrial water in lieu of this proposed project. Because of the anticipated population increase as a result of new deep mines adjacent to Maidsville, it is anticipated that additional municipal and industrial water supplies will be necessary about the time the multipurpose structure is completed. Cost estimates of the least expensive alternative to the multipurpose structure for

Exhibit 24-3. THACKERS RUN WATERSHED

Estimated Benefits by Measure

Item	Multipurpose Structure	Channel
Annual floodwater reduction benefits		
Residential	12%	88%
Commercial and industrial	0	100
Transportation and utilities	19.5	80.5
Crop and pasture	100	0
Other agriculture	100	0
Municipal water supply	0	100
Indirect	17	83
Savings in development costs	0	100
More intensive land use	100	0
Unemployed and underemployed labor resources	45	55
Municipal water supply	100%	0%

providing a municipal and industrial water supply indicate it would cost the local people approximately $950,000 at current prices. Annual operation, maintenance, and replacement costs to be incurred would be minimal and therefore will not be considered. This alternative would be financed by public debt with a coupon rate of 7 1/2 per cent. Equivalent benefits are provided by the multipurpose structure.

It is anticipated that the opening of deep mines adjacent to Maidsville will increase town population from the current 1,397 to about 3,000 within fifteen years. To accommodate the anticipated increase in population it is anticipated about 45C new homes and businesses will locate in or around Maidsville. It is expected that growth will be uniform at about thirty properties per year, beginning immediately. The terrain around Maidsville is characteristic of southwestern West Virginia with steep slopes surrounding narrow floodplains. Without the project, homes and businesses must, for the most part, locate on uplands that are expensive to develop or in the floodplain, which must be filled to meet local building codes. It is anticipated that an average of twenty properties per year will be built in the floodplain at an average savings in development costs of $4,000 per property at current prices if the structural measures are provided. Because development will occur in areas provided protection by the channel, these benefits are attributable to the channel.

An estimated 137 acres will have a more intensified agricultural use as a result of the project. This area is all located upstream of the channel and receives protection from the multipurpose structure. These benefits are expected to be approximately $6,500 annually throughout the life of the project and should begin accruing after five years from the completion of the multipurpose structure.

Maidsville is located in the Appalachian corridor, an area designated as having substantial and persistently high unemployment. Unemployed and underemployed labor will be used for construction of the multipurpose structure, channel works, and for road relocation upstream of the structure. It is estimated that 30 per cent of the construction and installation costs are labor-related and that approximately one third of the laborers to be used for construction and installation of the measures will be from among the previously unemployed. In addition, it is estimated that labor resource benefits to workers previously underemployed are about one fifth as much as the benefits to workers previously unemployed. Unemployed and underemployed labor resource benefits will accrue during the construction of the measures and road relocation. Expected price changes throughout the 100-year evaluation period are excluded from consideration in measuring future benefits and cost because (1) it is difficult to predict over such long periods, and (2) to anticipate a rate of inflation is to anticipate that the government will be ineffective in pursuing the national economic objective of price stability.

This project will be financed by public debt. No government bonds exist with a maturity that equals the 100-year projected life of the dam and channel works. The average coupon rate on government bonds with maturities greater than fifteen years is now 7 per cent. The average yield on government bonds with maturities greater than fifteen years is 8 per cent. The average cost of capital of private power companies and railroads is estimated to be 11 per cent. This can be thought of as the private sector opportunity cost of capital and includes a 3 per cent inflation premium and a 2 per cent risk premium.

QUESTIONS

1. Generate a table of net cash flows associated with the overall project in each year. You may assume that the life of all parts of the project is 100 years and that the benefits and expenditures will occur as follows:

Cash Flows	Years Occurring
Initial expenditures	as indicated in Exhibit 1
Operating, maintenance, and replacement expenditures	
on multipurpose structure	5–100
on channel	7–100
Net water supply benefits	4–100
Floodplain reduction savings	
from multipurpose structure	4–100
from channel	7–100
Savings on land development costs	7–15
More extensive land use	9–100

You may further assume that the new water supply benefits will total $70,992 per year (the $950,000 cost savings amortized over 100 years at 7.5 per cent) and that savings on land development will total $80,000 per year (twenty new properties per year times $4,000 per property) for the periods in which these benefits occur.

2. Calculate the net present value of the project and its internal rate of return. Justify the discount rate used in the net present value calculation.

3. On the basis of your response to Question 2, should the project be undertaken? Why or why not?

4. (At option of the instructor.) Why doesn't depreciation provide part of the cash flow for this project as it would in a corporate situation? Contrast this with the effect of depreciation on net cash flows for a profitable, income-taxed firm.

Do-It-Right Auto Repair

Capital Rationing

Darrell Archer's small incorporated business, Do-It-Right Auto Repair, was an outgrowth of his interests, experience, and schooling. As a teenager, he had been more than a bit car-crazy. He had purchased old cars and repaired them, he had raced go-karts, and in the summers he had worked at an auto repair garage. After high school, he had obtained a college degree in mechanical engineering, but he realized that he was not a theoretical type of person; he liked to work with machinery more than he did to design it.

In working for several gas station auto repair businesses, Archer had seen much of the slipshod and negligent practices that had given the business a bad name: delays, incompetence, and "fix-it-when-it-breaks" attitudes. Further, many repair businesses were equipped to handle only limited types of problems, and customers often had to take their cars to several specialized repair places to get them fixed. All these factors were quite annoying to customers. Darrell perceived, on the basis of the marketing courses he had taken as electives in college, that there was a relatively high-income market segment that would pay more to avoid these headaches of car ownership. He had set up his business to service that market segment. He guaranteed that vehicles in by 8 A.M. would be fixed by 5 P.M. the same day, unless he told the customer otherwise when the car was brought in (this restriction was necessary because some repairs took more than one day to complete). He hired only experienced, qualified, and honest mechanics. He fixed all auto-related problems except transmissions and bodywork. He did not sell gasoline. He located his facility near an upper-class neighborhood and kept the exterior of the building neat and clean. He sent postcards to regular customers when scheduled preventative maintenance (tuneups, tire rotation, and so on) was necessary. For a small fee, Archer would have customers' cars picked up from their houses at 8:30 A.M. and returned at 4:30 P.M. after repairs were completed. Cars were always washed before they were returned to customers (this cost the firm very little—it was done by a minimum-wage employee—but was much appreciated by customers). For all this quality and service, Archer charged 20 to 60 per cent more for similar repairs than did traditional garages.

The business had originally been financed by Archer's savings and a substantial loan from his father; a significant capitalization was required because the firm's policies required a higher inventory level and more equipment than did the average auto repair establishment. Because Archer did not want to take on any additional debt and would not consider selling stock, new equipment purchases and working capital contributions had to be funded from retained earnings. During the previous year, Archer had saved $50,000 from the business' cash flow for these purposes. He was considering investing in one or more of five independent projects:

Project 1: A New Towtruck.
Although Archer considered it a personal affront if one of his regular customers had an on-the-road breakdown, he did do some towing business. Net of sales revenues from his old truck, a new truck would cost $16,000 initially and was planned to have a four-year life. Cash flows had been forecast based on Archer's expectations regarding likely towing volumes and eventual trade-in value.

Project 2: Additional Electronic Analysis Equipment.
Archer believed that electronic analysis equipment would reduce mechanics' labor expenses and increase quality. The new equipment under consideration would cost $20,000 and would have a six-year life.

Project 3: Facilities Expansion
Expanding facilities would involve an addition to the firm's building and would give Archer the capability of servicing more business. It would require the entire $50,000 as an initial expense and would have a planned life of ten years.

Exhibit 25-1. DO-IT-RIGHT AUTO REPAIR

Net Cash Flows for Five Independent Projects (in Dollars)

Project/Year	0	1	2	3	4	5	6	7	8	9	10
1. Towtruck	-$16,000	$10,400	$ 7,800	$ 5,200	$ 7,600						
2. Analysis equipment	-20,000	14,700	8,800	7,800	5,900	3,900	1,900				
3. Facilities expansion	-50,000	15,100	14,200	13,300	12,400	11,500	10,600	9,600	8,700	7,800	6,900
4. Bodywork equipment	-10,000	3,500	3,200	2,800	2,400	2,700	1,700	1,400			
5. Computer	-$8,000	$ 2,000	$ 2,000	$ 2,000	$ 2,000	$ 6,000					

Project 4: Bodywork Equipment.
Such equipment would enable Archer to do some minor body-work (bent fenders, and so on); major crash damage would still have to be referred elsewhere. The initial cost was $10,000 and the life of the equipment was to be seven years.

Project 5: A Small-Business Computer.
Including word-processing equipment, exterior data storage, and similar peripherals, the total initial cost of a computer would be $8,000. This computer was to be used for word-processing, bill-ing, bookkeeping, and similar functions. It would save time and money and had a planned five-year life.

Expected net cash flows from each of these projects are pre-sented in Exhibit 25–1. All equipment was to be depreciated by accelerated methods. Archer's problem was to select the project or projects to be funded. He decided that they were all of a similar risk and that a 12 per cent discount rate was appropriate for net present value calculations. If any of the available $50,000 was left over, it was to be invested temporarily in a money market fund that yielded an after-tax return of 8 per cent to the company.

QUESTIONS

1. Calculate the net present values and profitability indexes for the five independent projects.

2. Rank the projects according to net present value and according to profitability index. Discuss any differences in rank-ing. Generate capital budgets for the firm on the basis of these ranking methods. Note that the five projects are indivisible (each must be adopted completely or not at all).

3. Are the capital budgets generated in response to Question 2 of maximum advantage to the firm? Why or why not? If not, generate an optimal budget.

4. (At option of the instructor.) Discuss Darrell Archer's limi-tation of investment funds for capital projects and its effect on the firm's income and value. Is this a common attitude among small businesses? Why or why not?

PART IV

Short- and Medium-Term Financing

Vance Corporation

Unsecured Short-Term Borrowing

Vance Corporation was a manufacturing firm located in Michigan. The firm had been started by the Vance family in 1967 and incorporated in 1976. The corporate form had been adopted to insulate the family's personal wealth from any possible claims against Vance Corporation. As of January 31, 1982 (the end of the firm's 1981 fiscal year), the firm had 66 employees, including five members of the Vance family. Dale Vance, the firm's founder, held the position of president. His sons, Roger and Joseph, were the firm's production manager and treasurer, respectively. John Clark and James Green, Dale Vance's sons-in-law, worked in the firm's shipping department.

Fiscal 1981 had been a reasonably good year for Vance Corporation; the firm had earned $55,648 after taxes on sales of about $1.3 million (see Exhibit 26-1 for the firm's balance sheet as of January 31, 1982 and statement of income for fiscal 1981). Although the economy was in a recession, Dale Vance expected the firm to have a modest increase in sales of about 10 per cent to $1,459,687. The nature of the firm's business was highly seasonal, however, and it was expected that 12 per cent of the firm's sales would occur in the first quarter, 30 per cent in the second quarter, 33 per cent in the third quarter, and 25 per cent in the fourth quarter. On the basis of these sales estimates, the firm's fixed asset acquisition plans, and the repayment schedule on the firm's current outstanding long-term debt, Joseph Vance had generated quarterly pro forma

Exhibit 26-1. VANCE CORPORATION

Financial Statements for the Fiscal Year Ending
January 31, 1982

Balance Sheet as of 1/31/82

Cash	$ 27,538	Accounts payable	$ 40,522
Accounts receivable	220,736	Due to bank, short-term	10,896
Inventory	46,030	Accrued wages	78,106
Prepaid expenses	9,568	Total current liabilities	129,524
Total current assets	303,872		
		Due to bank, long-term	44,288
Net fixed assets	128,782		
Other assets	6,040	Common equity	264,882
Total assets	$438,694	Total lia. and equity	$438,694

Income Statement for Fiscal Year Ending 1/31/82

Sales	$1,326,988
Wages	937,272
Materials	307,402
Interest	11,031
Earnings before taxes	71,283
Taxes	15,635
Earnings after taxes	55,648
Dividends	27,824
Additions to retained earnings	$ 27,824

income statements and balance sheets. These are presented in Exhibit 26-2.

Given the closely held nature of the firm, the nature of the firm's management and dividend policies might cause the outsider some confusion. During fiscal 1981, the firm had paid $27,824 in common share cash dividends to the family. This flow was double-taxed—once on the corporate level because federal income taxes had been paid before distribution, and once on the personal level (beyond the trivial personal dividend exemption for each recipient). If such a distribution was wanted, one might ask, why not increase the salaries of the owner-employees by a corresponding amount, which would be deductible on the corporate level? The reason such a strategy was not employed had to do with Internal Revenue Service rules. Under these rules, salaries of owner-employees could not be arbitrarily set; they must correspond to the duties of the employees and the salaries such duties would command in the marketplace. Thus the Vance family members could not have raised their own salaries beyond these marketplace limits to avoid corporate taxation of earnings without violating the law.

Exhibit 26-2. VANCE CORPORATION

Projected Quarterly Financial Statements for Fiscal 1982

Quarter Ending	Partial Income Statements 4/30/82	7/31/82	11/30/82	1/31/82
Sales	$175,162	$437,906	$481,697	$364,922
Earnings after taxes	7,357	18,392	20,231	15,327
Dividends	3,679	9,196	10,116	7,664
Additions to retained earnings	$ 3,678	$ 9,196	$ 10,115	7,663

	Balance Sheets			
Cash	$ 14,714	$ 36,784	$ 40,463	$ 30,653
Accounts receivable	116,308	290,770	319,847	242,308
Inventory	24,523	61,307	67,437	51,089
Prepaid expenses	9,807	10,046	10,285	10,524
Net fixed assets	132,002	135,222	138,442	141,672
Other assets	6,191	6,342	6,493	6,644
Total assets	$303,545	$540,471	$582,967	$482,890
Accounts payable	$ 21,720	$ 54,300	$ 59,730	$ 45,250
Due to bank, prior short-term	10,896	10,896	10,896	10,896
Accrued wages	41,338	103,346	113,680	86,122
Due to bank, prior long-term	42,045	39,832	37,619	35,406
Needed financing or (excess financing)	(81,014)	54,341	73,171	9,682
Common equity	268,560	277,756	287,871	295,534
Total liabilities and equity	$303,545	$540,471	$582,967	$482,890

The firm's formal debt arrangement consisted of short- and long-term arrangements with their local bank. The long-term debt consisted of a series of amortized term loans secured by specific fixed assets and backed by a security interest (a Uniform Commercial Code filing) against all the firm's other assets, existing or acquired thereafter. The average term of these loans was about five years. The bank was willing to make new loans of this type for up to 100 per cent of the book value of new fixed assets; during fiscal 1982, the firm intended to acquire about $20,000 in such assets. Interest rates on these new loans would be 21 per cent per year on an effective interest rate basis.

The firm's short-term line of credit was intended to cover seasonal financing needs, which were considerable given the nature of the business. The loan was unsecured, carried a stated interest rate of prime plus 1 1/2 per cent, and required a 15 per cent compensating balance. It was expected that the prime rate for fiscal 1982 would average 15 per cent. The loan agreement required that the loan balance be "cleaned up" for sixty days per year and limited maximum short-term borrowings on the agreement to $75,000. This cleanup was no problem for the firm, because sales made during the fourth fiscal quarter resulted in cash flows through collection of receivables during the following quarter (a slack period in terms of expenses), which could be used to pay off the loan.

Early in fiscal year 1982, Dale and Joseph Vance attempted to develop a debt financing plan for the fiscal year on the basis of Joseph's projections. They wanted to generate a plan that would fund the necessary balances most cheaply and keep the firm reasonably liquid. To maintain their ownership position, they ruled out selling new stock. It was agreed that a current ratio at the end of the quarter of at least 1.85 to 1 should be maintained, even during periods of maximum funds demand (the end of second and third quarters), if possible. They ruled out secured short-term borrowing because of the nature of the firm's long-term debt arrangements. Besides borrowing more on a long-term basis and/or continuing with the currently existing short-term arrangement, another alternative was to temporarily forgo the discount on bills due to several suppliers. Currently, the firm purchased about one half of its materials on terms of 2 per cent ten days, net thirty days, and the balance on net thirty-day terms. The firm, as a policy matter, discounted the former bills, but used its bargaining power to obtain informal extended payment terms from firms billing in the latter fashion. As of January 31, 1982, these net thirty bills were being paid in an average of eighty-five days.

QUESTIONS

1. Assuming that the balance to be financed is borrowed on the short-term bank credit line when financing is needed, calculate the firm's projected current ratio and total debt to total assets ratio at the end of fiscal 1981 and at the end of each quarter for fiscal 1982. Ignore for this question only the maximum borrowing constraint. Discuss trends and fluctuations in these ratios and the reason for their occurrence.

2. Discuss the advantages and disadvantages of financing the firm's short-term financing requirements using various portions

of short-term interest-bearing debt and long-term interest-bearing debt financing. Be sure to discuss the effects of such decisions on future earnings per share, given the uncertainty involved in forecasting sales.

3. Calculate the effective yearly interest rate on the firm's short-term credit line and on the option of forgoing the discount and delaying payment to suppliers billing on 2 per cent ten net thirty days term. State any assumptions as to how long payments would be delayed if the discount is forgone.

4. Develop a financing plan for the firm for fiscal 1982 on the basis of interest costs and other considerations.

5. (At option of the instructor.) It is often said that the dividend and financing decisions are intimately linked. Discuss this idea in connection with Vance Corporation. Generate and discuss quarterly pro formas, financing requirements, and TD/TA ratios for the alternatives of (a) a 75 per cent dividend payout, and (b) a 0 per cent dividend payout.

6. (At option of the instructor.) Although the yield curve is usually upsloping, downsloping yield curves do occur. Discuss how this would affect the firm's decisions regarding the proportions of short- and long-term debt financing used, including the tradeoffs involved.

Transformers, Inc.

Secured Short-Term Borrowing

Transformers, Inc. was a manufacturer of transformers, generators, and similar electrical devices. Founded in the early 1950s, the firm had had substantial success until the early 1970s when a series of problems beset the company. The recession of 1970 and 1971 had a severe effect on sales. From fiscal year 1969 to fiscal year 1970, the firm's sales declined by 33 per cent (see Exhibit 27-1 for the firm's financial statements for the fiscal years ending December 31, 1969 through December 31, 1972). Sales remained at these reduced levels during fiscal 1971, then recovered in 1972. However, the losses during 1970 and 1971, which totaled $691,066, had put a severe strain on the firm's financial position. To partly finance the losses, the firm had borrowed heavily from a bank during this period, and the burden of interest expenses on the firm's profits had risen dramatically. The bank had indicated that it would not be receptive to requests by Transformers, Inc. for new unsecured financing. Yet, in order to support expected increases in sales in upcoming years, the firm would need some source of short-term funds.

Besides these difficulties, Transformers, Inc. was also having problems with its trade suppliers. Many of the raw materials used by the firm had to be ordered increasingly in more substantial quantities. The reasons were that some domestic suppliers offered substantial price reductions for ordering in large quantities (quantity discounts), making ordering in small lots uneconomical, and some overseas suppliers required that the firm take large shipments of materials at once, because they did not maintain warehouse facilities in the United States. Because of its strained financial position and heavy investment in inventories, Transformers, Inc. had been forced to pay suppliers' invoices well beyond their terms of sale. In early 1973, there was a real possibility that some of these suppliers would refuse to make further shipments, which could result in severe production problems for the firm.

In light of these problems a credit manager of one of the firm's suppliers suggested to Roger Trexler, the treasurer of Transformer's Inc., that the firm consider some type of secured short-term financing. Trexler contacted the firm's bank officer and found him receptive to this suggestion. The banker also proposed to Trexler, who was not familiar with this type of lending, that a financing system of this type could also be used to replace some of the firm's short-term borrowings (on which the firm was paying 7 per cent above the prime rate) with a lower-interest loan arrangement. However, given the firm's current financial position, the banker said that a general security agreement with regard to inventory or accounts receivable would not be sufficient. An independent company would have to monitor the collateral and perform certification services for the bank. This sounded expensive to Trexler, but he made an appointment to discuss the matter with the agent for the company that usually performed collateral monitoring and certification services for the bank. At the meeting, the agent presented details of two borrowing plans that seemed reasonable to Trexler: certified accounts receivable and field warehousing of inventory.

Under the certified accounts receivable system, the collateral monitoring and certification services company would first examine the receivables of Transformers, Inc. to see if these were good collateral. If these were approved as collateral, the bank would then prepare a security agreement, have it signed by Transformers, Inc., and have it filed under applicable law. Payments against secured receivables would then be made by customers to a special collateral bank account. The collateral monitoring and certification services company would then serve to verify balances and prepare reports of balances eligible as collateral for secured loans (usually receivables more than ninety days old were not considered to be good security). The bank would then loan to Transformers, Inc. up to 75 per cent of the certified and monitored balance. In return for its services, the collateral monitoring and certification services company required a fee of 2 1/2 per cent of the amount of the loan. How-

Exhibit 27-1. TRANSFORMERS INC.

Balance Sheets and Income Statements, Fiscal Years 1969–1972 (Ordered by the Accountant's Method)

Fiscal year ending	12/31/1972	12/31/1971	12/31/1970	12/31/1969
Cash	$ 17,975	$ 5,297	$ 76,753	$ 103,545
Accounts receivable	494,484	509,829	451,615	472,008
Inventory[1]	1,613,364	882,457	916,312	741,951
Other current assets[2]	184,869	183,308	391,148	344,995
Total current assets	$2,310,692	$1,580,891	$1,835,828	$1,662,499
Net property, plant, and equipment	1,874,369	1,909,177	1,708,438	1,199,262
Other assets[3]	562,571	510,851	376,253	223,229
Total assets	$4,747,632	$4,000,919	$3,920,519	$3,084,990
Accounts payable	734,941	771,894	669,945	214,807
Due to bank—short-term	812,274	375,882	130,289	12,139
Total current liabilities	$1,547,215	$1,147,776	$ 800,234	$ 226,946
Due to bank—long-term	646,201	797,106	642,783	169,122
Deferred income taxes	0	0	135,190	76,370
Common stock	46,547	39,041	36,605	36,350
Paid in capital	1,841,909	1,474,140	1,354,775	1,342,280
Retained earnings	665,760	542,856	950,932	1,233,922
Owner's equity	$2,554,216	$2,056,037	$2,342,312	$2,612,552
Total lia. & O.E.	$4,747,632	$4,000,919	$3,920,519	$3,084,990

	1969	1970	1971	1972
Sales	3,259,708	2,176,716	2,090,918	3,170,860
Cost of sales [4]	2,693,799	2,259,640	2,094,805	2,361,388
Gross margin on sales	565,909	(82,924)	(3,887)	809,472
Selling & admin. expense	464,363	520,404	436,342	542,359
Interest expense	12,300	38,924	108,882	138,005
Income from operations	89,246	(642,252)	(549,111)	129,108
Other income	0	53,066	0	53,083
Earnings before taxes	89,246	(589,186)	(549,111)	182,191
Taxes	48,902	(306,196)	(141,035)	59,287
Earnings after taxes	40,304	(282,990)	(408,076)	122,904
Dividends	0	0	0	0
Contribution to R.E.	$ 40,304	$ (282,990)	$ (408,076)	$ 122,904

[1] Inventory breakdown at lower of cost or market for 1972:

Raw materials	$1,332,959
Work in process	105,011
Finished goods	185,394
Total inventory	$1,613,364

[2] Other current assets including tax claims, equipment for resale, and prepaid expenses.

[3] Other assets including development costs, notes due the firm, and similar miscellaneous items.

[4] Components of cost of sales by years:

	1972	1971	1970	1969
Direct labor	$ 448,664	$ 377,065	$ 474,524	$ 538,760
Direct materials	1,652,972	1,445,416	1,604,344	1,885,659
Other	259,752	272,324	180,772	269,380
Total CGS	$2,361,388	$2,094,805	$2,259,640	$2,693,799

ever, the loan, secured by receivables, would carry an interest rate of 4 per cent over prime rather than the current 7 per cent over prime.

Under the field warehousing arrangement, the collateral monitoring and certification services company would first inspect and verify the quality of the inventory as loan collateral. For Transformers, Inc. it was expected that only raw materials inventory, which had a reasonable resale value, would meet collateral qualifications. The security agreement would then be executed and filed on the inventory, and the collateral monitoring and certification services firm would lease (for a nominal fee) the appropriate portion of the storage area of the plant of Transformers, Inc. Access to this area would then be restricted (by use of a locked fence), and the collateral monitoring and certification services firm would train and arrange for the bonding of personnel to control materials flow to and from the restricted area and prepare periodic reports to the bank on the value of the collateral. The bank would loan to Transformers, Inc. up to 60 per cent of the collateral balance. The field warehousing fee to the collateral monitoring and certification services firm was to be $2,000 per year plus 1 1/2 per cent of the amount of the loan. Bank interest charges would be the same as for the certified receivables system. If either secured financing system was adopted, the bank was expected to require that 30 per cent of the new loan proceeds were to be used to retire part of the old, unsecured short-term loan balance due the bank. This requirement was to compensate the bank for dilution of its unsecured interest, because receivables or inventory were to be pledged and would not be available to directly satisfy unsecured claims.

QUESTIONS

1. Calculate the following ratios for Transformers, Inc. from the fiscal years ending 12/31/69 through 12/31/72:
   a. Debt ratio (total debt/total assets).
   b. Interest expense as a per cent of sales.
   c. Current ratio.
   d. Quick ratio.
   e. Inventory turnover ratio.
   f. Average collection period.
   g. Accounts payable turnover ratio (direct materials expense/ accounts payable).

Discuss the trends in these ratios relative to the problems of Transformers, Inc. as outlined in the case.

2. Calculate the effect on earnings after taxes for 1973 of (a) the certified accounts receivable collateral system, and (b) the field warehousing system of inventory collateral. You may assume that average accounts receivable and inventory balances would be $600,000 and $1,800,000, respectively; that the maximum amount of the loans will be outstanding for the entire year; and that 1973 would be a profitable year for the firm. State any other assumptions.

3. Which collateral system would be of most advantage to Transformers, Inc. if one or the other must be chosen? Why?

4. Discuss some advantages of financing sales patterns with borrowings against accounts receivable and/or inventory as opposed to using some longer-term financing, such as an amortized intermediate-term loan.

5. (At option of the instructor.) Discuss some other ways in which a firm such as Transformers, Inc. could obtain short-term funds by using current assets as security.

Reynolds' Machine Shop

Bank Borrowing

Reynolds' Machine Shop, located in western Pennsylvania, had been established by John Reynolds in 1962 and incorporated in 1965. The firm was engaged in general metalwork, including stamping, grinding, and machining. Like most machine shops, the firm's plant was set up in a job shop design, with all lathes in one part of the building, drill presses in another, and so forth. Although this layout created considerable problems with inventory handling, it was necessary because of the nature of the business. Reynolds' Machine Shop was engaged in producing and repairing machine and equipment parts on an order-to-order basis for machinery manufacturers. Run sizes were usually small, and production processes varied from part to part; thus an assembly-line setup could not be justified.

Reynolds had gradually built the business up, increasing sales and profits each year. In 1974, the firm grossed $658,130 in sales and made $32,048 in net profit (see Exhibits 28-1 and 28-28-2 for the firm's balance sheet and income statement for fiscal 1974). However, the increasing volume of sales had put severe strains on the firm's working capital. Reynolds had kept his accounts payable current for most of the year only by borrowing relatively large amounts on the firm's short-term bank credit line. This was one of the firm's two borrowing arrangements with the bank; the other was a series of intermediate-term loans for the purchase of specific pieces of equipment. The short-term line of credit was intended to finance seasonal fluc-

Exhibit 28-1. REYNOLDS' MACHINE SHOP

Balance Sheet as of 12/31/74

Cash	$ 962	Due banks short-term	$ 53,987
Accounts receivable	70,042	Accounts payable	27,132
Inventory	91,721	Acc. taxes	16,246
Total C.A.	$162,725	Other accruals	51,851
		Total C.L.	$149,216
Net fixed assets	$134,517	Due on term loans	11,801
Other assets	6,056	Common stock*	20,000
	$303,298	Retained earnings	122,281
		Total lia. & OE	$303,298

*Owned by Reynolds and his relatives.

tuations and was personally guaranteed by Reynolds; the term loans were secured by the specific pieces of equipment that these loans had been used to purchase. As with most seasonal loans, the short-term credit line included the provision that the loan be cleaned up (paid off) for sixty days during the year. In early 1975, Reynolds realized that in order to clean up the short-term loan during the coming year he would either have to curtail sales to hold down receivables and necessary inventories or stretch out payables to lengths that he knew would not be acceptable to suppliers. Neither option seemed desirable. He arranged a meeting with William Hanley, loan officer at Western Pennsylvania Citizens Bank (WPCB), to describe and discuss the problem.

Hanley knew that WPCB had been seeking new local loan business. Reynolds had been a customer at the bank for more than ten years and had always honored loan agreements in the

Exhibit 28-2. REYNOLDS' MACHINE SHOP

Income Statement for Fiscal 1974

Sales	$658,130
Cost of sales	473,854
Gross margin	184,276
Selling, admin., dep., and int.	138,493
EBT	45,783
Federal & state taxes	13,735
EAT	32,048
Dividends	10,000
Cont. to ret. earnings	$ 22,048

past. The obvious solution was to convert the short-term line of credit into some type of longer-term unsecured loan guaranteed by Reynolds; John Reynolds had suggested a $75,000 amount and a five-year term as appropriate figures. This would supplant the firm's balance on the short-term credit line and provide needed additional cash to finance the firm's expected sales growth of 7 per cent per year. However, Hanley wondered about the safety of the loan and whether it could be paid off in the suggested five-year term.

QUESTIONS

1. Typical ratios for firms of similar business line and size to Reynolds' as of late 1974 were as follows:

Current ratio	1.5
Quick ratio	1.0
Total debt to net worth	1.3
Accounts receivable turnover	7.4
Inventory turnover (based on cost of sales)	7.5
Total asset turnover	2.1
Profit before taxes/net worth	26.1%
Profit before taxes/total assets	7.5%
Profit before taxes/sales	5.8%

Compute these ratios for Reynolds' Machine Shop as of December 31, 1974 and assess the firm's liquidity, financial leverage, asset management, and profitability. Relative to similar firms, was Reynolds' Machine Shop a good credit risk?

2. Construct pro forma statements for Reynolds' for each of the fiscal years ending December 31, 1975 through December 31, 1979. You may assume that cash remains at the level reached after the application of the loan funds; that the short-term bank loan is terminated; that taxes will remain the same per cent of earnings before taxes; that net fixed assets, common stock, dividends, other assets, and amount due on the old term loans remain at December 31, 1974 levels; and that all other entries (except retained earnings, of course) can be forecast on a per cent of sales basis. The balance on the new loan will be the reconciling item. On the basis of these pro formas, will the loan be paid off in the five-year term?

3. If you were the bank loan officer, would you grant the loan? Why or why not?

4. (At option of the instructor.) Besides the interest rate and term of a loan, loan agreements generally contain some restrictive covenants. Suggest and justify several of these that Hanley might want to include in any intermediate-term loan agreement with Reynolds' Machine Shop.

HCM Corporation

Lease Versus Borrow and Buy (1)

HCM Corporation (formerly Heavy Construction and Manufacturing Corporation) was founded around the turn of the century to do specialized construction work for the steel industry. Prior to 1965, the firm was still dependent on its steel plant construction business; this part of the company's operations accounted for 45 per cent of annual earnings. Steel plant construction was a cyclical business that had a destabilizing effect on the firm's growth prospects. In the late 1960s and early 1970s, the firm made a conscious effort to deemphasize this business area, and in the late 1970s the firm had become a diversified manufacturer engaged in numerous operations, including road materials production, road construction, and the production of chemical preservatives. Construction work for the steel industry had been reduced to 10 per cent of total sales. With hundreds of domestic and overseas locations and sales in the billions of dollars, the firm was one of the 500 or so largest basic industry companies in the world.

One of the firm's largest divisions produced materials for road construction. This division had about 150 operating locations and marketed materials in twenty states. More than 70 per cent of sales were from aggregates (such as crushed stone, sand, and gravel), concrete, and paving services. The balance was from sales of asphalt and asphalt-related products. All these materials were of low intrinsic value, and transportation was an important factor in production cost. Markets for aggregates were localized and confined to areas near the firm's quarries. Some of these materials (in particular, stone and sand products) were transported from the quarries to road construction sites by diesel-powered highway tractors. In early 1979, one of the division's locations submitted to corporate headquarters a request to obtain four such tractors with a purchase price of $56,400 per tractor. A capital budgeting analysis showed that the tractors should be obtained; thus the question concerned the best way to finance the acquisition.

One financing arrangement involved entering into a capital lease with the firm that produced the tractors, which offered such leases through a financing subsidiary. This lease arrangement, which would last four years (the useful life of the tractors to HCM), would entail payment of $20,683 per tractor the first year, $18,957 the second year, $17,231 the third year, and $15,228 the fourth year, the payments due at year-end.* The effect of the investment tax credit would be passed on to HCM. Any salvage value would, of course, go to the firm providing the lease.

Another alternative was to purchase the tractors, finance them by a term loan, and scrap them after four years. There was some difficulty, however, in obtaining a good estimate of the salvage value of the tractors after four years. Originally, the division had estimated a salvage value of 30 per cent of the purchase price, or $16,920 per tractor. Upon reconsideration, however, it was decided that $11,280 (20 per cent of the purchase price) might be more reasonable. The firm decided to depreciate the tractors to the latter value by the sum-of-years-digits method. HCM's marginal tax rate was 50 per cent. An inquiry to HCM's principal bank disclosed that the going rate of interest on such term loans was 12 per cent. Service to the tractors, whether they were financed by term loan or lease, was to be provided by HCM.

QUESTIONS

1. Calculate the net present value of the leasing alternative for the four tractors.
2. Calculate the net present value of the term loan alternative for the four tractors.
3. Which financing method should be chosen? Why?

---

*Payments in the actual situation were on a monthly basis. They have been converted here to a yearly basis to save students' calculation time.

4. Suppose that the expected salvage value of the tractors was the $16,920 per tractor amount originally estimated rather than the $11,280 amount on which the firm eventually settled. How would this affect the net present value of the term loan alternative and your decision?

5. (At option of the instructor.) Discuss some other considerations regarding the relative merits of leasing versus financing with a term loan that might influence HCM's decision between these alternatives.

Bovery Products, Inc.

Lease Versus Borrow and Buy (2)

Bovery Products, Inc. was a medium-sized, diversified manufacturer of consumer goods and had been a leader in the adoption of computer technology in all phases of its business. In the
1950s, Bovery had been one of the first firms to obtain a bulky,
tube-type computer for use in bookkeeping and accounting
functions. As computer hardware and software progressed, the
firm quickly adopted each new innovation, although not without thorough investigation of the technical aspects of each bit
of emerging technology. Because of its extensive experience in
the area of computerization, Bovery's management was able to
bring new systems on line with a minimum of disturbance and
trouble to existing operations. Careful shopping among hardware and software suppliers, domestic and foreign, was relied
upon to keep costs down. Bovery credited its superior inventory
control, accurate market forecasts, efficient management of
financial resources, and excellent customer service to its extensive use of the computer. Thus, when a capital expenditure request for an additional $2 million in computer hardware was
made by the data services department in early 1976, it was not
unexpected that this would be approved.

A question arose, however, as to how the new equipment
would be financed. In the past, as a matter of policy, the financial management of Bovery had relied on term loans to finance
intermediate-term assets of this sort. However, the supplier of
this particular hardware also offered a leasing package, and the

financial executives of Bovery were in disagreement as to how to handle the alternatives (see Exhibit 30-1 for details of all the alternative financing plans). In a meeting on February 2, 1976, with the president of the firm, William Black, the firm's financial vice-president, had urged that any financing alternative be evaluated by the standard net present value method.

"There is no reason to deviate here from standard financial analysis techniques," Black said. "All the cash flows associated with the leasing and borrowing alternatives are easily calculated. It is true that for the term loan alternative we have to make principal payments and take out a service contract, but we get the benefits of the depreciation, the investment tax credit, and the salvage value. For the lease alternatives, our cost is only the after-tax lease expense. I don't see where the debate lies."

Brian Perry, Black's assistant, took a different view. "I hate to disagree with you, Bill, but there is a factor I don't believe you have considered. There are advantages to leasing beyond the mere cash flows involved. By avoiding borrowing, we keep our debt ratio down and make our financial structure appear

Exhibit 30-1. BOVERY PRODUCTS, INC.

Details of Three Financing Plans

Plan I: Lease available from vendor

Length of lease: 8 years
Salvage value: goes to vendor
Investment tax credit: goes to vendor
Service contract: service provided by vendor
Yearly payments: $275,000 before taxes

Plan II: Lease available from commercial leasing firm

Length of lease: 8 years
Salvage value: goes to leasing firm
Investment tax credit:
  leasing firm will pass on benefit to Bovery in terms of reduction
  of first year's lease payment
Service contract: service contract to be purchased by leasing firm
Yearly payments: $235,000

Plan III: Amortized term loan from Bovery's bank

Length of loan: 8 years
Salvage value: goes to Bovery
Investment tax credit: goes to Bovery
Service contract: must be purchased by Bovery; before tax cost,
  $30,000 per year
Yearly payments: based on 9 per cent amortized loan

less risky. This keeps the price of our stock up and the costs of borrowing down. Also, the leased assets will not appear on our balance sheet, but we can use them to support operations, with favorable implications for our total asset turnover and fixed asset turnover ratios. By improving these ratios, we make the firm seem more productive, again with positive implications for our stock price. That's why I solicited another proposed lease arrangement from a commercial leasing firm in addition to the seller's leasing plan; I believe that these effects of leasing on stock price are so important that we want to be able to use leasing if at all possible. Isn't one of the goals of financial management to raise the price of the firm's stock?"

Black retorted somewhat hotly, "There is no doubt that raising the price of our stock is always a good idea, but the securities market is not so easily fooled as you imply. We report lease commitments and expenses in our annual report, and any security analyst with the brains of a snapping turtle could ferret out this deception by computing our fixed charge coverage ratio and taking a close look at the footnotes. I don't believe your arguments have any bearing on the matter."

At this point Black and Perry agreed to leave the matter for future resolution and go on to some specifics on the project. It was agreed that the expected salvage value of the hardware eight years hence was $500,000 according to the data service department's best estimates of inflation and obsolescence. Given the riskiness of this cash flow, it was agreed that a 15 per cent discount rate was appropriate. Other cash flows, such as lease payments, principal payments, and similar flows, were considered more deterministic, and it was agreed that the appropriate discount rate for these flows was 4 per cent. The firm's tax rate was 48 per cent.

QUESTIONS

1. Calculate the net present value of each of the financing plans. For the term loan option, you may assume that the firm uses the sum-of-years-digits depreciation method and that an investment tax credit of 10 per cent of the purchase price is available to offset income in the period in which the purchase is made.

2. Which financing option should be undertaken? Why?

3. (At option of the instructor.) On the basis of available knowledge, assess Black's and Perry's arguments regarding the effect on stock price of leasing versus borrowing.

PART V

Long-Term Financing, the Cost of Capital, and Dividend Decisions

Matthews Industries, Inc. (A)

Effects of Bond/Stock Decisions on Earnings per Share (1)

Matthews Industries, Inc., with headquarters in Milwaukee, was engaged primarily in manufacturing valves and meters to measure and control flow rates of fluids and gases. These products were used basically in heavy industry: petroleum and natural gas exploration and refining, chemical production, and the like. The firm also provided field service for its products and had a division devoted to this service function. Sales were usually in the United States and Mexico, but the firm had done some business in the Middle East and had provided products to Britain in association with the development of the North Sea oil field.

In the early 1970s, Matthews Industries had embarked on a series of acquisitions and expansions. In 1971, the firm acquired a pump manufacturer and distributor in Kentucky. In 1974, the firm had formed a division to produce larger, computer-controlled metering systems. In 1977, two acquisitions were another pump manufacturing firm and a firm that produced machinery for the natural gas industry. Also during the 1970–1977 period several other operations of Matthews Industries expanded.

To finance these expansions and acquisitions, the firm in the early 1970s relied primarily on cash flows from operations. To fully utilize these cash flows, stock dividends had been partially substituted for cash dividends in the fiscal years 1974 to 1977. As a result, the firm's dividend payout ratio (cash dividends divided by net income) had fallen from 13.8 per cent in fiscal

Exhibit 31-1. MATTHEWS INDUSTRIES, INC.

Balance Sheets as of Fiscal Year End, 1973 to 1977 (Fiscal Year Ends September 30; in Rounded Thousands; Ordered by the Accountant's Method)

Year Ending	9/30/77	9/30/76	9/30/75	9/30/74	9/30/73
Cash	$ 1,278	$ 881	$ 2,250	$ 1,927	$ 482
Cert. of deposit	2,400	2,040	0	0	0
Accounts receivable	17,288	14,021	11,425	9,286	6,977
Inventories	26,792	20,873	23,586	17,170	10,675
Other cur. assets	596	935	1,860	282	1,862
Total cur. assets	48,354	38,750	39,121	28,665	19,996
Prop., plant, and equipment	34,348	24,322	19,074	14,918	12,498
Accumulated dep.	8,015	6,607	5,530	4,742	4,043
Net fixed assets	26,333	17,715	13,544	10,176	8,455
Other assets	2,077	200	671	160	238
Total assets	76,764	56,665	53,336	39,001	28,689
Current portion LTD	1,519	154	5,594	2,582	4,850
Accounts payable and accrued expenses	12,582	10,635	7,236	6,688	4,672
Income taxes due	7,398	3,770	2,069	2,960	629
Other current lia.	1,241	1,379	4,976	1,480	0
Total current lia.	22,740	15,938	19,875	13,710	10,151
Long-term debt	12,484	6,050	6,199	4,235	824
Deferred taxes	2,088	1,324	1,081	692	685
Common stock	8,066	7,006	6,086	5,174	4,500
Capital surplus	20,110	12,883	8,149	4,358	3,098
Retained earnings	11,276	13,464	11,946	10,832	9,431
Owners' equity	39,452	33,353	26,181	20,364	17,029
Total lia. and OE	$76,764	$56,665	$53,336	$39,001	$28,689

1973 to 8.8 per cent in fiscal 1977, despite sharply rising earnings. In 1977, however, the two acquisitions made it necessary for the firm to borrow $7 million from a bank. Although this was shown as an increase in long-term debt on the firm's September 30, 1977 balance sheet, it was understood that this $7 million was to be repaid early in fiscal 1978. See Exhibits 31-1 and 31-2 for the firm's balance sheets and income statements for the fiscal years ending September 30, 1973 through September 30, 1977.

Late in fiscal 1977, George Livengood, treasurer of Matthews Industries, was trying to decide whether this money and an additional $3 million for future expansion of the firm could best

Exhibit 31-2. MATTHEWS INDUSTRIES, INC.

Statements of Income and Retained Earnings for Fiscal Years 1973–1977 (Fiscal Year Ends September 30; in Rounded Thousands; Ordered by the Accountant's Method)

Year Ending	9/30/77	9/30/76	9/30/75	9/30/74	9/30/73
Net sales	$ 85,824	$ 85,754	$ 73,076	$ 49,871	$ 36,568
Cost of goods sold	51,164	53,164	45,938	29,672	23,364
Gross margin	34,660	32,590	27,138	20,199	13,204
Selling, admin. and other expenses	21,619	18,625	16,711	12,917	10,135
Earnings before interest and taxes	13,041	13,965	10,427	7,282	3,069
Interest on LTD	1,118	798	1,056	560	310
Earnings before taxes	11,923	13,167	9,371	6,722	2,759
Income Taxes	5,248	5,600	4,056	3,120	1,218
Net Income	6,675	7,567	5,315	3,602	1,541
Retained Earnings, Beginning Year	13,464	11,946	10,832	9,431	8,102
Cash dividends	584	407	300	262	212
Stock dividends	8,279	5,642	3,901	1,939	0
Retained earnings, end year	11,276	13,464	11,946	10,832	9,431
Year-end shares outstanding, adjusted for stock dividends	3,223,741	3,220,616	3,145,302	3,145,102	3,099,919
Net income per share (based on year-end shares)	$2.07	$2.35	$1.69	$1.15	$0.50
Average price per share	$24.06	$17.34	$12.27	$6.89	$4.95

be obtained through the issue of additional common stock (as the firm had done in 1968) or by the private placement of bonds with an institutional investor. He was concerned primarily with the impact of the decision on future earnings per share. In an attempt to assess this impact, he first made several financial projections and estimates for the firm for fiscal 1978. Although sales had been stagnant between fiscal 1976 and 1977, fiscal 1978 was expected to be a reasonably good year for the firm in terms of dollar sales volume. Livengood decided to assign probabilities of 0.2 to sales growth of 5 per cent, 0.3 to sales growth of 7 per cent, 0.3 to sales growth of 9 per cent, and 0.2 to sales growth of 11 per cent, on the basis of economic and industry forecasts. He estimated selling, administrative, and other expenses at $25 million. Once the $7 million in interim bank debt was paid off, he expected interest expense on the firm's long-term debt (exclusive of interest on new issues) to be $800,000. He decided to assume that cash dividends would be raised to $700,000 and that stock dividends would be discontinued.

Inquiries to an investment banker had disclosed several facts about potential new issues. Because the firm's stock was trading near the high end of its trading range as of late fiscal 1977, the firm could be expected to net (after flotation) $26 per new common share issued. Twenty-five year bonds, due in 2003, could be placed with an institutional investor at a coupon rate of 9 1/4 per cent with a negligible flotation cost.

QUESTIONS

1. Generate estimates of the firm's earnings per share for the bond and stock financing options for each sales level for fiscal 1978. State any necessary assumptions.

2. Calculate the expected earnings per share and the coefficient of variation of earnings per share for fiscal 1978 for the stock and bond financing options.

3. Calculate, or obtain graphically, the breakeven sales figure on earnings per share between the stock and bond financing options for fiscal 1978.

4. On the basis of the data generated in response to Questions 1 to 3, which financing option should be chosen? Why?

5. (At option of the instructor.) Generate pro forma statements of liabilities and owners' equity for September 30, 1978 on the basis of the *expected* level of sales and income under the

bond and stock financing options. State all assumptions. Assuming that the optimal capital structure for a firm in the involved industry is in the range of 40 to 50 per cent debt (total debt/total assets), how does this affect your decision between bond and stock financing?

Original Chemical Company (B)

Effects of Bond/Stock Decisions on Earnings Per Share (2)

Original Chemical Company was a publicly owned firm with common shares traded on the New York Stock Exchange. The firm had been started in the 1920s and had grown internally until the mid-1960s. Between 1966 and 1975, the firm acquired several smaller chemical companies, usually through an exchange of common stock, although a cash exchange was sometimes involved. Fourteen firms, domestic and foreign, were acquired during this period. These acquisitions enabled Original Chemical to broaden considerably its line of chemicals into several business areas in which the firm had no previous dealings: detergents, certain plastics, and petrochemical products. In 1976, however, the firm withdrew from the retailing end of the petrochemical business by selling its forty gasoline service stations and decided to concentrate on the production and sale of industrial chemical products.

In 1979, the firm produced and sold a broad line of chemicals for industrial use, including specialty chemicals, commercial petroleum products, and plastics. Because of its long experience in the chemicals industry and considerable technical expertise, the firm did substantial business in products formulated to meet customer specifications. The firm maintained fifteen domestic manufacturing locations and a similar number of research and applications laboratories. The majority of the firm's six foreign subsidiaries were consolidated on the firm's balance sheet,

Exhibit 32-1. ORIGINAL CHEMICAL COMPANY (B)

Consolidated Balance Sheets as of December 31 (Rounded Thousands of Dollars; Ordered by Accountant's Method)

	1979 (preliminary)	1978	1977
Cash and marketable securities	$ 27,107	$ 18,761	$ 11,600
Accounts receivable	67,951	60,349	52,631
Inventories	56,946	49,804	44,592
Prepaid expenses and other CA	2,730	2,645	3,496
Total CA	154,734	131,559	112,319
Gross property, plant, and equipment	220,050	212,830	198,230
Accumulated depreciation	111,906	103,172	94,977
Net property, plant, and equipment	108,144	109,658	103,253
Investment in nonconsolidated affiliates	5,215	4,988	6,941
Excess of acquisition cost over book value of acquired firms	10,030	10,090	10,244
Other assets	4,430	6,877	7,902
Total assets	282,553	263,173	240,659
Notes payable to bank	4,070	2,687	3,378
Accts. payable to trade creditors	52,927	48,583	41,625
Dividends payable	1,795	1,640	1,409
Income taxes payable	3,054	3,143	220
Total current liabilities	61,846	56,053	46,632
Long-term debt	55,448	57,770	59,420
Deferred credits	21,323	19,110	16,652
Common stock ($5 par)	22,878	22,477	21,939
Capital surplus	3,355	2,679	2,884
Retained earnings	117,703	105,084	93,132
Total stockholders' equity	143,936	130,240	117,955
Total Liabilities and Owner's Equity	$282,553	$263,173	$240,659

which is presented as Exhibit 32-1. Income statements are presented in Exhibit 32-2.

In early 1980, Ms. Joan Laio, a financial analyst for the firm, projected the amount that the firm would have to borrow on a note basis from the bank during that fiscal year (this forecast is the essence of Original Chemical Company (A), Case 5). She then submitted her forecast to the firm's financial vice-president, Thomas Upham, along with supporting documentation.

Exhibit 32-2. ORIGINAL CHEMICAL COMPANY (B)

Consolidated Statements of Income and Retained Earnings for Fiscal Years Ending December 31 (Rounded Thousands of Dollars; Ordered by Accountant's Methods)

	1979 (preliminary)	1978	1977
Net sales	$505,930	$452,766	$422,187
Cost of sales	410,917	365,476	347,702
Selling and administrative expenses	44,277	39,182	35,050
Depeciation, depletion, and amortization	13,863	12,121	11,093
Interest expense	4,330	4,321	4,918
Operating income	32,543	31,666	23,424
Other income	2,314	1,968	3,722
Other expenses	0	0	0
Earnings before taxes	34,857	33,634	23,706
Income taxes	15,142	15,154	11,093
Earnings after taxes	19,715	18,480	12,613
Dividends on common stock	7,096	6,528	5,640
Contributions to retained earnings	$ 12,619	$ 11,952	$ 6,973

The firm made these bank borrowings on an interim basis between new security issues so that it could eventually make larger issues and save money on flotation costs. On receiving Ms. Laio's forecast, Upham decided that it might be time to consider a new securities issue, rather than postponing this for another year. To lower flotation costs, Upham decided on a large issue, compared to the firm's prior securities issues, designed to net the firm $40 million. He planned to use the revenues from this issue to clean up the balance on the firm's note account with the bank, to pay off a portion of outstanding long-term debt, and to finance future asset expansion. He asked Ms. Laio to do further analysis on the effects of bond and stock financing on the firm's earnings per share for 1980. He believed that the best long-term debt financing alternative for the firm might be a 9 1/2 per cent sinking fund debenture due in twenty years; another chemical company had recently issued such a debenture, and the issue had sold well. He knew that his firm's stock was then trading at about $29 per share, but would have to be priced for sale, net of flotation costs, at $27 per share to sell the issue quickly.

Ms. Laio had previously estimated a sales growth of 7.66 per cent from fiscal 1979 to fiscal 1980, but she knew that economic conditions were quite uncertain. On the basis of data from the regression equation used to generate the growth forecast and her insight into economic conditions, she approximated the probability distribution of sales levels with a discrete distribution:

Level	Probability
A Actual sales equal to forecast	60%
B Actual sales $40 million more than forecast	15%
C Actual sales $40 million less than forecast	15%
D Actual sales $80 million more than forecast	5%
E Actual sales $80 million less than forecast	5%

As in her previous analysis, Ms. Laio decided to assume that depreciation for 1980 would total $9.2 million; that other non-cash expenses for 1980 would total $5.7 million; and that other income for 1980 would total $2 million. She decided to revise downward her forecast of interest expenses on previously issued debt. According to Upham's debt retirement plans, she now expected this to total $4 million for 1980.

QUESTIONS

1. Generate forecasts of earnings per share and degree of financial leverage for each sales level for the bond and stock financing options for Original Chemical Company for fiscal 1980.

2. Calculate the expected earnings per share and coefficient of variation of earnings per share for the bond and stock financing options for Original Chemical Company for 1980.

3. Graph earnings per share versus sales volume for the bond and stock financing options. From this graph, obtain the breakeven point between the two financing options based on sales volume.

4. On the basis of your answers to Questions 1 to 3, which financing option should be chosen? Why?

5. (At option of the instructor.) Was early 1980 a good time to do long-term financing using *either* option? Why or why not? How might this affect Upham's final decision and his negotiation of the indenture provisions of the bond issue, if this is used?

Matthews Industries, Inc. (B)

Effects of Issuing Various Securities on Earnings per Share

Matthews Industries, Inc., with headquarters in Milwaukee, was a firm engaged primarily in manufacturing valves and meters to measure and control flow rates of fluids and gases. These products were used basically in heavy industry: petroleum and natural gas exploration and refining, chemical production, and the like. The firm also provided field service for its products, with a division devoted to this service function. Most sales were in the United States and Mexico, but the firm had done some business in the Middle East and had provided products to Britain in association with the development of the North Sea oil field.

In the early 1970s, Matthews Industries had embarked on a series of acquisitions and expansions. The firm in 1971 acquired a pump manufacturer and distributor in Kentucky. In 1974, the firm formed a division to produce larger computer-controlled metering systems. In 1977, two acquisitions were made: another pump manufacturing firm and a firm producing machinery for the natural gas industry. Also during the 1970–1977 period several other operations of Matthews Industries were expanded.

To finance these expansions and acquisitions, the firm in the early 1970s relied primarily on cash flows from operations. In order to fully utilize these cash flows, stock dividends had been partially substituted for cash dividends in the fiscal years 1974 to 1977. As a result, the firm's dividend payout ratio (cash dividends divided by net income) had fallen from 13.8 per cent in fiscal 1973 to 8.8 per cent in fiscal 1977, despite sharply rising earnings. In 1977, however, the two acquisitions made it necessary for the firm to borrow $7 million from a bank. Although this was shown as an increase in long-term debt on the firm's September 30, 1977 balance sheet, it was understood that this $7 million was to be repaid early in fiscal 1978. See Exhibits 33-1 and 33-2 for the firm's balance sheets and income statements for the fiscal years ending September 30, 1973 through September 30, 1977.

Late in fiscal 1977, George Livengood, treasurer of Matthews Industries, considered the problem of how this money and an

Exhibit 33-1. MATTHEWS INDUSTRIES, INC. (B)

Balance Sheets as of Fiscal Year-End, 1973 to 1977 (Fiscal Year Ends September 30; in Rounded Thousands; Ordered by the Accountant's Method)

Year Ending	9/30/77	9/30/76	9/30/75	9/30/74	9/30/73
Cash	$ 1,278	$ 881	$ 2,250	$ 1,927	$ 482
Cert. of deposit	2,400	2,040	0	0	0
Accounts receivable	17,288	14,021	11,425	9,286	6,977
Inventories	26,792	20,873	23,586	17,170	10,675
Other cur. assets	596	935	1,860	282	1,862
Total cur. assets	48,354	38,750	39,121	28,665	19,996
Prop., plant, and equipment	34,348	24,322	19,074	14,918	12,498
Accumulated dep.	8,015	6,607	5,530	4,742	4,043
Net fixed assets	26,333	17,715	13,544	10,176	8,455
Other assets	2,077	200	671	160	238
Total assets	76,764	56,665	53,336	39,001	28,689
Current portion LTD	1,519	154	5,594	2,582	4,850
Accounts payable and accrued expenses	12,582	10,635	7,236	6,688	4,672
Income taxes due	7,398	3,770	2,069	2,960	629
Other current lia.	1,241	1,379	4,976	1,480	0
Total current lia.	22,740	15,938	19,875	13,710	10,151
Long-term debt	12,484	6,050	6,199	4,235	824
Deferred taxes	2,088	1,324	1,081	692	685
Common stock	8,066	7,006	6,086	5,174	4,500
Capital surplus	20,110	12,883	8,149	4,358	3,098
Retained earnings	11,276	13,464	11,946	10,832	9,431
Owners' equity	39,452	33,353	26,181	20,364	17,029
Total lia. and OE	$76,764	$56,665	$53,336	$39,001	$28,689

Exhibit 33-2. MATTHEWS INDUSTRIES, INC.

Statements of Income and Retained Earnings for Fiscal Years 1973–1977 (Fiscal Year Ends September 30; in Rounded Thousands; Ordered by the Accountant's Method)

Year Ending	9/30/77	9/30/76	9/30/75	9/30/74	9/30/73
Net sales	$ 85,824	$ 85,754	$ 73,076	$ 49,871	$ 36,568
Cost of goods sold	51,164	53,164	45,938	29,672	23,364
Gross margin	34,660	32,590	27,138	20,199	13,204
Selling, admin. and other expenses	21,619	18,625	16,711	12,917	10,135
Earnings before interest and taxes	13,041	13,965	10,427	7,282	3,069
Interest on LTD	1,118	798	1,056	560	310
Earnings before taxes	11,923	13,167	9,371	6,722	2,759
Income Taxes	5,248	5,600	4,056	3,120	1,218
Net Income	6,675	7,567	5,315	3,602	1,541
Retained Earnings, Beginning Year	13,464	11,946	10,832	9,431	8,102
Cash dividends	584	407	300	262	212
Stock dividends	8,279	5,642	3,901	1,939	0
Retained earnings, end year	11,276	13,464	11,946	10,832	9,431
Year-end shares outstanding, adjusted for stock dividends	3,223,741	3,220,616	3,145,302	3,145,102	3,099,919
Net income per share (based on year-end shares)	$2.07	$2.35	$1.69	$1.15	$0.50
Average price per share	$24.06	$17.34	$12.27	$6.89	$4.95

additional $3 million for future expansion of the firm could best be obtained. His initial analysis concerned the effects of financing with new bonds or new stock on the firm's earnings per share for the next year (fiscal 1978; this analysis is the essence of Matthews Industries, Inc. (A), Case 31). He presented this analysis to the firm's president, who, although he liked the methodology, considered the analysis to be excessively limited. The president suggested to Livengood that he extend the analysis to three years in the future, that he consider several additional security financing methods, and that he look explicitly at the effects of issuing various securities on the firm's capital structure. After consultation with the firm's investment bankers, Livengood developed four financing alternatives:

1. *New Common Stock.* The firm had used a common stock issue in 1968. The firm's stock was currently selling at $29, but it was expected that the firm would net $26 per new share after flotation expenses.

2. *New Bonds.* Twenty-five year bonds, due in 2003, could be placed at a coupon rate of 9 1/4 per cent with negligible flotation cost.

3. *Preferred Stock.* This issue of preferred stock would be perpetual, nonparticipating, and callable. The coupon rate would be $4.00 per year; the issue would be placed with institutional investors to net Matthews Industries $47 per share (par on the preferred would be $50).

4. *Bonds with Warrants.* Here, warrants would be attached to the bonds as a "sweetener." Twenty-five-year, $1,000 bonds with ten warrants attached to each bond could be sold at an 8 1/2 per cent coupon rate with negligible flotation. The warrants would allow the purchase of common stock at a $32 price.

Livengood initially questioned the selling price on the new preferred, which implied an 8 per cent yield, lower than bond yields for a more risky issue. The investment banker explained that the preferred dividends would be 85 per cent tax exempt and therefore provide a 7.4 per cent return to the corporate institutional investor in the 48 per cent tax bracket. For the 9 1/4 per cent bond issue, the after-tax return for an investor in a similar bracket would be only 4.9 per cent. Because investors make decisions on the basis of after-tax yields, this argument satisfied Livengood.

Although sales had been stagnant between fiscal 1976 and 1977, fiscal 1978 and beyond were expected to be reasonably good years for the firm in terms of dollar sales volume. Livengood decided to assign probabilities of 0.2 to future sales growth of 5 per cent, 0.3 to future sales growth of 7 per cent, 0.3 to future sales growth of 9 per cent, and 0.2 to future sales growth of 11 per cent, on the basis of economic and industry forecasts. He estimated selling, administrative, and other expenses at $25 million for fiscal 1978; he expected this expense class to grow at a rate of 6 per cent per year. Once the $7 million in interim bank debt was paid off, he expected interest expense on the firm's long-term debt (exclusive of interest on any new issues) to be $800,000. He assumed that total cash dividends to common stock, if the new common stock financing option was used, would be $700,000 in fiscal 1978, $756,000 in fiscal 1979, and $816,000 in fiscal 1980. If other financing options were used, he expected these dividends to be proportionately smaller. He also expected, with this raise in common cash dividends, that stock dividends would be discontinued.

QUESTIONS

1. Generate estimates of the firm's earnings before taxes and new interest for the growth rates mentioned in the case and for the fiscal years 1978, 1979, and 1980. State all necessary assumptions.

2. Calculate the expected earnings per share, coefficient of variation of earnings per share, and expected book long-term debt to total capitalization ratios for each of the financing alternatives for each of the fiscal years 1978, 1979, and 1980. You may assume that share price grows at the same rate as sales and that warrants are exercised when share price passes exercise price. State all other necessary assumptions.

3. On the basis of your analysis for Question 2, which of the four financing methods should the firm use? Why?

4. (At option of the instructor.) When they do their public financing by security sale, firms generally aggregate several years' needs and make one large security issue of a specific type of security. Why is such a methodology used? Detail the advantages and disadvantages to Matthews Industries of issuing a combination of the four options listed in the case to obtain the necessary funding; use the traditional capital structure arguments in your analysis.

ABC Meat Locker, Inc.

Computing the Cost of Capital (1)

The Reckart family of Baltimore, Maryland, who had been successful butchers for three generations, ran a well-established retail and commercial meat business. However, when Bob Reckart
earned his MBA from the University of Pennsylvania in 1960,
he had bigger plans for the family-owned firm. During the
1960s and early 1970s, he expanded the firm to provide two
new lines: frozen foods for airline meals and relatively large
quantities of freezer-ready beef to families at near wholesale
prices. He also convinced his family to change the firm's name
to ABC Meat Locker. By 1979, the firm was grossing $15 mil-
lion per year in sales and young Reckart had become president.
He was not ready, however, for the new ideas presented to him
by his cousin, Sharon Reckart, when she joined the firm fresh
from a midwestern college. In particular, she wanted to calculate the firm's marginal, weighted average cost of capital and
use this rate in connection with the firm's capital budgeting
procedures. Matters came to a head at a meeting in January
1980.

"I agree that the concept is valid," the president said, "but
how can we apply it to a family-held firm? Our securities aren't
publicly traded; we own the stock and the bank holds the debt."

"This is a problem with the methodology, but we can get
around it," Ms. Reckart replied. "Several of our competitors
are publicly traded, and we can get some information on this
basis, although we are a much smaller firm than any of the

others in our industry. The most comparable firm I've been able to find, on the basis of product mix, sales, asset size, and capital structure, is Herbert Foods. Its product mix is similar to ours, and its capital structure contains about the same proportion of debt and equity as ours—58 per cent equity and 42 per cent debt based on their market value weights. However, its sales and assets are about 170 per cent of ours. Incidentally, the debt/equity mix that Herbert Foods and we use is very close to the average debt/equity mix for our industry. Herbert Foods earned about twenty cents per share last year and its stock is selling for $1.50 per share. This stock is traded on the over-the-counter market. It will probably pay ten cents per share in cash dividends during 1980. This dividend has been rising fairly steadily; it was only five cents per share five years ago. Like us, Herbert Foods has no preferred stock outstanding. It just announced the private placement of a new issue of bonds with an insurance company; the coupon rate was 12 1/2 per cent."

"Okay," Reckart responded, "take a whack at it and see what you come up with. However, you had better be able to justify whatever you calculate."

The next day, the young woman started to calculate the marginal, weighted average cost of capital for ABC Meat Locker by using and adjusting data on publicly traded Herbert Foods. Because her family's firm was so small, she decided to assume a 10 per cent flotation on any new common stock. This high flotation was based on the idea that any new stock issues would have to be privately placed with investors by a dealer in venture capital, and such dealers usually had commissions of this magnitude. She also knew that her firm was expected to have about $1 million in earnings available for reinvestment during the coming year.

QUESTIONS

1. Calculate the marginal, weighted average cost of capital using both internal and external equity sources for the relevant equity portions for ABC Meat Locker as of early 1980 on the basis of the information in the case. State all assumptions.

2. Generate a graph relating the firm's marginal, weighted average cost of capital to the size of its capital budget through the first discontinuity in this function. Explain how this would be used, along with rate of return and initial cost data on the firm's possible investments, to make capital budgeting and divi-

dend decisions, assuming that all possible capital projects are of the same risk as the firm's average project.

3. (At option of the instructor.) Should book values be used in calculating the capital structure weights for ABC Meat Locker? Why or why not?

Union Carbide Corporation*

Computing the Cost of Capital (2)

In 1978, Union Carbide Corporation was one of the world's largest chemical companies, with sales of $8 billion. Although the vast majority of the firm's products were used in industry, many of the company's developments had directly affected consumers. These included the development and/or commercialization of polyethylene, a widely used plastic, and of ethylene glycol antifreeze. In 1978, about 68 per cent of the firm's sales were within the United States, with the remaining 32 per cent in foreign sales. The firm's operations were divided into five industry segments: chemicals and plastics, gases and related products, metals and carbons, batteries and home products, and specialty products.

Chemicals and Plastics
(37 per cent of the firm's 1978 sales). In this industry segment, chemical feedstocks were used to produce products for many industries, including agriculture, textiles, cosmetics, automotive products, and electronics. This segment had 1978 sales of $2.91 billion, operating profit of $309 million, and assets of $3.2 billion.

*This case was prepared from public information. It is designed for educational purposes and not for research or to illustrate the correct or incorrect handling of administrative practices.

Gases and Related Products

(16 percent of the firm's 1978 sales). In this segment, the firm produced numerous commercial gases (oxygen, nitrogen, and others) that were distributed in tank trucks or cylinders. Also included were Union Carbide's activities in the areas of welding materials, wastewater treatment, and cryogenics. This segment had 1978 sales of $1.26 billion, operating profit of $167 million, and assets of $1.3 billion.

Metals and Carbons

(18 per cent of the firm's 1978 sales). Included were what might be termed the firm's "heavy" businesses: producing and selling chromium, magnesium, silicon, tungsten, vanadium, uranium, and carbon products. Much of the output of these businesses went to the steel industry. This segment had 1978 sales of $1.42 billion, operating profit of $166 million, and assets of $1.4 billion.

Batteries and Home and Automotive Products

(17 per cent of 1978 sales). Unlike most of the firm's other businesses, this segment's outputs went almost directly to consumers. Flashlights, batteries, and similar products were produced under the familiar Eveready trade name; plastic wrap and bags under the Glad trade name; antifreeze under the Prestone trade name; and automotive wax and specialty products under the Simoniz trade name. This segment had 1978 sales of $1.36 billion, operation profit of $178 million, and assets of $800 million.

Specialty Products

(12 per cent of the firm's 1978 sales). Here were several areas of business not elsewhere classified, including the production of some agricultural products, electronic products, medical products, and food-related products. This segment had 1978 sales of $930 million, operating profits of $48 million, and assets of $800 million.

Businesses in these five industry segments had not performed equally well in fiscal 1978, nor were the trends and fluctuations in margins similar among groups (see Exhibit 35-1 for a chart of operating returns by industry segment for several years). In dollar terms, the sales in all five industry segments had risen over fiscals 1974 to 1978, but dollar profits had fallen for the Chemicals and Plastics and Metals and Carbons segments, remained almost the same for the Specialty Products segment,

Part V: Long-Term Financing, the Cost of Capital, and Dividends

Exhibit 35-1. UNION CARBIDE CORPORATION

Operating Return for 1978 and Operating Margin for 1974-1978 Ratios by Industry Segment

	Chemi-cals & Plastics	Gases & Related	Metals & Carbons	Batteries, Home, Auto	Spe-cialty Products
Operating profit/ assets (1978)	9.7%	12.8%	11.9%	22.2%	6.0%
Operating profit/ sales (1974)	23.0	13.5	20.7	15.1	10.2
Operating profit/ sales (1975)	13.3	15.4	20.2	15.1	11.9
Operating profit/ sales (1976)	11.5	15.5	17.6	10.8	8.0
Operating profit/ sales (1977)	10.2	13.5	16.3	12.2	6.8
Operating profit/ sales (1978)	10.6%	13.3%	11.7%	13.1%	5.2%

Source: Computed from figures on page 4 of Union Carbide 1978 Annual Report.

and had risen for the Gases and Related Products and Batteries and Home and Automotive Products segments.

Exhibit 35-2 provides an income statement for fiscal 1978 and a balance sheet as of December 31, 1978 for the firm. As of the same date, the firm had no preferred stock outstanding; average common share price for 1978 (average of high and low prices) was $38.44; and an average of 64,799,000 common shares were outstanding. The firm's long-term debt at that time consisted of numerous issues. Among the largest were two issues of sinking fund debentures: a 7.50 per cent issue due in 2006, with a book value of $200 million, and an 8.50 per cent issue due in 2005, with a book value of $300 million. In 1978 these two issues traded at an average price of $891.88 and $980.00, respectively, per $1,000 in par value. Exhibit 35-3 presents historic data on several financial statistics regarding the firm.

QUESTIONS

1. Compute the marginal cost of capital using internal and external equity to fund the equity portions for Union Carbide as of late 1978. Use book weights and plot the costs of capital

Exhibit 35-2. UNION CARBIDE CORPORATION

Financial Statements for Fiscal 1978

Income Statement for Fiscal 1978 (Rounded Millions)

Net sales	$7,870
Cost of sales and distribution expense	5,580
Research and development	156
Selling, administrative, and other expenses	943
Depreciation	417
Interest	159
Other income and expenses	(12)
Income before provision for income taxes	627
Provision for income taxes	206
Income of consolidated companies	421
Less: Minority stockholder's share of income	32
Plus: Firm's share of other companies carried at equity	5
Net income	394
Dividends declared	181
Additions to retained earnings for 1978	$ 213

Balance Sheet as of 12/31/78 (Rounded Millions)

Cash	$ 109
Time deposits and short-term marketable securities	175
Notes and accounts receivable	1,259
Inventories (total)	1,541
Prepaid expenses	154
Total current assets	3,238
Plant, property, and equipment less depreciation	4,119
Total other assets	218
Total assets	7,866
Accounts payable	434
Short-term debt	338
Current portion of long-term debt	54
Accrued income and other taxes	220
Other accrued liabilities	571
Total current liabilities	1,616
Long-term debt	1,483
Deferred credits	848
Minority interest in unconsolidated subsidiaries	281
Common stock	522
Retained earnings	3,118
Less: Treasury stock	(1)
Total liabilities & stockholders' equity	$7,866

Source: Union Carbide's 1978 Annual Report, pp. 28 and 29.

Part V: Long-Term Financing, the Cost of Capital, and Dividends

Exhibit 35-3. UNION CARBIDE CORPORATION

Annual Statistics for Several Items 1969-1978

	Sales ($/share)	Net Income ($/share)	Div. ($/share)	Div. Payout Ratio	Total Assets ($/share)
1969	48.496	3.08	2.000	65%	55.49
1970	50.039	2.60	2.000	77	58.93
1971	50.150	2.52	2.000	79	58.55
1972	53.700	3.40	2.000	59	61.11
1973	64.710	4.89	2.075	42	68.40
1974	87.192	8.61	2.175	25	79.97
1975	92.360	6.23	2.400	39	95.60
1976	102.703	7.15	2.500	35	107.17
1977	109.031	6.05	2.800	46	115.03
1978	120.951	6.09	2.800	46%	120.90

Source: Taken or computed from data provided in the Union Carbide 1978 Annual Report, page 23 (dividend payout ratio computed from net income and dividend columns).

on a graph versus the size of the capital budget. You may assume (1) that flotation costs on new common shares would be 2 per cent of the market value of the issue; and (2) that the firm would first utilize depreciation-shielded funds and then other funds sources in funding its capital budget. State any necessary additional assumptions, including those related to the cost of debt, the long-term growth rate of dividends, and flotation on new debt.

2. Should the calculated cost of capital be used as a discount rate for net present value calculations or as a cutoff for internal rate of return for projects within each industry segment without adjustment? Why or why not? If not, what adjustments need to be made?

3. (At option of the instructor.) Assume that the beta for Union Carbide's common stock is 0.9 and that the security market line as of late 1978 could be described by the equation:

$$\text{required return} = .08 + 4(\text{beta})$$

Calculate the marginal cost of capital for Union Carbide as of late 1978 using the Capital Asset Pricing Model to estimate the shareholders' required rate of return on equity.

4. (At option of the instructor.) Assuming that the interest rate based on the book value of the firm's long-term debt

averages 6.63 per cent, and that this long-term debt currently sells to yield a simple before-tax rate averaging 8.20 per cent, calculate the firm's costs of capital using internal and external equity to fund the equity portions using market value weights. As component costs, use those calculated in response to Question 1.

Diagnostic Products Corporation*

Going Public

In early June 1982, Diagnostic Products Corporation and its shareholders announced the intention to sell 700,000 shares of common stock. Before that time, there had been no public market for shares of the firm. Of the shares offered, 417,100 were to come from the firm and 282,900 were to come from current shareholders. After the offering, a total of 3,583,100 shares would be outstanding. Publicly held shares would then be traded over the counter under the NASDAQ symbol *DPCZ*.

The firm, with headquarters in Los Angeles, was organized as a California corporation in 1971. The revenues of the firm were derived from the manufacturing and marketing of medical test kits. These test kits utilized an immunological response system to assess the presence of substances in a patient's body fluids. The body's immune system responds to the presence of foreign substances, such as viruses and parasites. These foreign substances, which are called antigens, trigger the production of antibodies. The antibodies bind to the antigens and start a process to eliminate their effects. Antibodies are specific in that each type of antibody attacks only the corresponding type of antigen. Thus, by observing the effects in a body fluid of a particular antibody, one can imply the presence or absence, and extent, of

*This case was prepared from public information. It is designed for educational purposes and not for research or to illustrate the correct or incorrect handling of administrative practices.

corresponding antigens. This is useful in the diagnosis and/or treatment of several medical conditions, including pregnancy, anemia, and cancer.

The firm's kits contained the materials to perform a specific test. The materials generally included an antibody, certain chemical reagents, and standards and data necessary to assess test results. In early 1982 the firm produced two general types of such kits, differentiated by the types of reagents involved. In radioimmunoassay (RIA) diagnostic kits, radioactive tracers were used, whereas enzymeimmunoassay (EIA) kits utilized enzymes. Because of the short shelf life of such kits (typically eight to ten weeks for one of the firm's RIA kits), products were shipped to recipients by air from Los Angeles International Airport.

The first RIA kits had been marketed in 1969, and between 1970 and 1981 expenditures on these products had risen from virtually nothing to more than $485 million worldwide. This growth was mirrored by the company's expanding sales and profits picture; some of these data are presented in Exhibit 36-1. The dip in net income per share in fiscal 1980 was pri-

Exhibit 36-1. DIAGNOSTIC PRODUCTS CORPORATION

Selected Income Statement Data*

Year Ended December 31,

	1977	1978	1979	1980	1981
Net revenues	$2,037	$3,753	$4,927	$7,048	$9,400
Cost of sales	553	836	1,176	1,974	2,769
Selling expense	455	624	723	1,170	1,793
Research and development	113	173	334	785	1,264
General and administrative	452	615	830	930	1,092
Income before income taxes	464	1,486	1,914	1,945	2,475
Net income	251	745	987	984	1,376
Net income per share	$ .09	$ .26	$ .34	$ .33	$ .45

*Source: "Diagnostic Products Corporation 700,000 Shares Common Stock Prospectus," page 7.

marily the result of expenses related to the firm's move into new and larger quarters, which were expensed in the year incurred. In 1982 the firm manufactured 44 different diagnostic kits that were used to perform 28 different tests; these were sold worldwide in fifty-six countries, with foreign sales accounting for 54 per cent of fiscal 1981's revenues.

The market for test kits of this sort was quite competitive; at the time, there were more than fifty suppliers of such kits, although the ten largest (which included Diagnostic Products) accounted for about three fourths of domestic sales. Technical innovations, as in many high-technology markets, were quite frequent. Consequently, Diagnostic Products Corporation's well-being depended on technological advancement. As a result, 24 per cent of its staff and 13 per cent (in fiscal 1981) of its revenues were devoted to research and development. Probably the two biggest areas of research and development activities by the firm in 1982 were (1) the development of new products for detection of substances, and (2) the development and production of monoclonal antibodies. The latter work was in connection with a new type of antibody production which, it was believed, would result in more accurate diagnostic tests.

The firm's last balance sheet before the share offering is presented in Exhibit 36-2. The new shares were to be sold at an offering price of $12 each, to yield the firm $11.12 after underwriting discounts and commissions. Additional expenses to the firm were expected from the share sale of about $265,000 so that the firm would net about $4,373,000 from the sale of the 417,100 shares. These proceeds were to be used to repay bank debt and to increase the firm's working capital. In all probability, the working capital contribution would be temporarily invested in marketable securities until needed for corporate purposes. A major portion of the funds from the sale of shares by existing shareholders would go to the repayment of the "note receivable from partnership," which was the result of a sale-and-leaseback transaction of the firm's land and buildings from the firm to a partnership involving several shareholders. This money also was to go toward increasing the firm's working capital. After the share sale, officers and directors of the corporation would still hold 1,266,200 shares. Although the balance sheet as of March 31, 1982 showed a declared dividend of $32,000, the prospectus related to the stock offering stated, "The Company does not intend to pay cash dividends in the foreseeable future so that it can reinvest its earning in the development of its business."

Exhibit 36-2. DIAGNOSTIC PRODUCTS CORPORATION

Consolidated Balance Sheet as of March 31, 1982*

Cash	$ 70,000	Short-term bank	
Marketable securities	1,000	note	$ 650,000
Accounts receivable		Accounts payable	519,000
(net)	2,001,000	Accruals	358,000
Inventory	2,020,000	Dividends declared	32,000
Prepaid expenses	68,000	Income taxes	
Deferred income tax		payable	383,000
benefit	107,000	Total current	
Total current assets	4,267,000	liabilities	1,942,000
Machinery, equipment,		Deferred income	
net of depreciation	1,573,000	taxes	635,000
Other assets	51,000	Deferred gain on	
Note receivable from		sale/leaseback	84,000
partnership	1,448,000	Common equity	4,678,000
Total assets	$7,339,000	(3,156,000 shares	
		outstanding)	
		Total lia. and	
		equity	$7,339,000

*Abstracted from "Diagnostic Products Corporation 700,000 Shares of Common Stock Prospectus," pp. 31 and 32.

QUESTIONS

1. Calculate the firm's current ratio, quick ratio, and ratio of total debt to total assets as of March 31, 1982. Generate a pro-forma balance sheet, applying the revenues from the sale of shares as indicated in the case and ignoring any other changes between March 31, 1982 and the receipt of these funds. Recalculate the three ratios for this pro forma statement; discuss any changes. What is likely to happen to these ratios during the period soon after the funds are received? Why?

2. Calculate the total flotation expense to the firm as a percent of the issue. Contrast this with average flotations on common share issues as tabulated in J. F. Weston and E. F. Brigham, *Essentials of Managerial Finance*, 5th ed., 1979, page 488, or similar texts. Discuss any differences with reference to the role of the underwriter in new issues of this type.

3. Calculate the percent of shares that will be owned by officers and directors of the corporation after the security issue. Is this still effective control? Why or why not?

4. One of the most difficult problems in selling shares of a firm to the public when the firm's stock has not previously been traded is establishing an offer price. Calculate (1) the book value per share as of March 31, 1982; (2) a hypothetical market value per share as of January 1982 based on the dividend capitalization model; and (3) a hypothetical market value per share as of January 1982 based on an estimated price earnings ratio. Contrast the three results with the actual offering price. (For the dividend capitalization model, a shareholder's required return is needed. This must be higher than the firm's before-tax cost of debt, which was 15.2 per cent as of December 31, 1981.)

5. (At option of the instructor.) Discuss the firm's projected capital structure position after the application of the funds from the security issue relative to the firm's likely optimum debt/equity proportions. Be sure to include such considerations as the firm's future sales growth rate, sales stability, competition, and asset structure in your discussion of the firm's optimal position.

Florida Coast Banks, Inc.*

Financing with Convertible Securities

Florida Coast Banks, Inc., was a bank holding company formed in 1970. The original name of the firm was Florida Bancorp; the new name had been adopted in 1976. By 1979 the firm existed primarily as a holding company for its four subsidiary firms: a data processing subsidiary (FBC Systems, Inc.) and three banking subsidiaries. The three banking subsidiaries included two federally chartered banks: Florida Coast Bank of Coral Springs, N.A. (with a main office and three branches) and Florida Coast Bank of Palm Beach County, N.A. (located in Boca Raton), and one state-chartered bank: Florida Coast Bank of Pompano Beach (with a main office and three branches). Some of these banks and branches had been acquired by the exchange of stock and others had been established by the firm. In March 1979, the firm was the twenty-third largest of thirty multi-bank holding companies in the state of Florida on the basis of total assets and deposits (see Exhibits 37-1 and 37-2 for financial data).

The subsidiary banks were all commercial banks with an emphasis on retail banking. Trust services were also provided by the Florida Coast Bank of Pompano Beach for customers of all the banking subsidiaries wanting this service. Of the approximately $145 million in loans (before unearned discounts and

*This case was prepared from public information. It is designed for educational purposes and not for research or to illustrate the correct or incorrect handling of administrative practices.

Exhibit 37-1. FLORIDA COAST BANKS, INC.

Abbreviated Statements of Consolidated Financial Position and
Consolidated Income for Fiscal Year Ending 12/31/78

Cash and due from banks	$ 25,233,544
Securities held (at cost)	54,571,571
Loans (less unearned discount and reserves)	135,985,003
Federal funds sold and securities purchased under resale agreement	1,350,000
Premises and equipment	5,702,537
Other assets	3,164,367
Total assets	226,007,022
Demand deposits	89,178,715
Savings deposits	61,090,652
Time deposits	47,246,911
Federal funds purchased and securities sold under repurchase agreement	8,300,000
Other liabilities	1,698,153
Notes payable (long-term)	7,207,500
Total liabilities	214,721,931
Common stock (par $1)	1,123,668
Capital surplus	5,213,208
Retained earnings	4,948,215
Total stockholders' equity	11,285,091
Total liabilities and owners' equity	226,007,022
Interest income on loans, securities, and federal funds sold and purchased	16,681,995
Interest expense	7,219,321
Provision for loan losses	1,297,500
Net interest income after loan loss provision	8,165,174
Other operating income (trust department fees, service charges, etc.)	1,259,686
Other operating expenses (salaries, benefits)	7,711,508
Income before taxes and security gains	1,713,352
Provision for income taxes	370,164
Security gains less related taxes	7,062
Net income	$ 1,350,250

reserves), which the banking subsidiaries had outstanding as of December 31, 1978, about 20 per cent were secured by one- to four-family residential properties, about 20 per cent were other real estate loans, about 10 per cent were commerical and industrial loans, and about 47 per cent were loans to individuals for household, family, and personal expenditures. The remaining 3 per cent were divided among other loan categories. During 1978, the firm earned interest on assets at an average rate of 9.45 per cent, whereas the average rate paid on sources of funds was 6.15 per cent, for an interest margin of 3.30 per cent.

Exhibit 37-2. FLORIDA COAST BANKS, INC.

Some Yearly Data, Fiscal Years 1974-1978

Fiscal Year	1974	1975	1976	1977	1978
Cash dividends per share	$.40	$.40	$.40	$.25	$.22
Return on average equity	8.91%	10.02%	9.31%	5.51%	12.51%
Net income per share	$.73	$.78	$.75	$.43	$1.20
Net equity per share*	$8.20	$8.23	$8.65	$8.99	$9.60
Equity to assets ratio	6.0%	6.2%	5.9%	5.6%	5.1%
Stock trading price†	$9.88	$6.25	$5.75	$5.55	$6.55

*Book value of stockholder's equity divided by average number of common shares outstanding

†1974 to 1976: average of yearly high and low bid prices; 1977 and 1978: average of quarterly high and low bid prices. On 8/28/79, the closing representative bid price as reported by NASDAQ was $7.625.

As of May 31, 1979, the firm's long-term debt consisted of four issues: an issue of 9.40 per cent notes due in 1989 with a balance of $1.5 million outstanding; an issue of 9.75 per cent notes due in 2002 with a balance of $1.25 million outstanding; an issue of 9.80 per cent notes due in 2002 with a balance of $3.25 million outstanding; and a floating rate term loan with $1.17 million outstanding. The last issue originated in mid-1978, when the balance of $1,345,000 on an existing rotating credit line was converted into a term loan. The terms of this loan were changed in April 1979, and the interest rate on the loan was changed to 116 per cent of the prime rate plus 1/2 per cent; interest on this loan as of March 31, 1979 was at 12 1/2 per cent. The repayment schedule for this issue included payments through 1983.

Although the firm's earnings had risen substantially from fiscal 1977 to fiscal 1978, cash dividends on common shares had not been raised. The annual report of the firm for 1978 stated, "Your directors continue to maintain a conservative cash dividend policy for the purpose of retaining earnings in capital accounts to support the substantial growth we are undergoing."* The firm's common stock was traded on the over-the-counter market.

*"Florida Coast Banks, Inc., 1978 Annual Report," page 3.

Exhibit 37–3. FLORIDA COAST BANKS, INC.

Redemption Prices for Convertible Preferred Stock

Issue to 8/15/80	$11.00	8/16/84 to 8/15/85	$10.50
8/16/80 to 8/15/81	$10.90	8/16/85 to 8/15/86	$10.40
8/16/81 to 8/15/82	$10.80	8/16/86 to 8/15/87	$10.30
8/16/82 to 8/15/83	$10.70	8/16/87 to 8/15/88	$10.20
8/16/83 to 8/15/84	$10.60	8/16/88 to 8/15/89	$10.10
		8/16/89 and after	$10.00

On August 30, 1979, an announcement appeared in the *Wall Street Journal* indicating an offer of new securities of Florida Coast Banks, Inc. The offer involved 600,000 shares of a new class of stock: convertible preferred. The stock was priced to sell at $10 per share and was to yield $1 in yearly cash dividends per share, payable quarterly. Each share of this new issue was convertible into one share of the firm's common stock; nondilution provisions were included. The issue was callable by Florida Coast Banks, Inc., at redemption prices varying with the time outstanding (the redemption prices are provided in Exhibit 37–3). This issue had no sinking fund but did carry the right to elect two additional corporate directors if six quarterly dividends were unpaid. The sale of the convertible preferred issue was expected to net the firm $5,580,000 after underwriting discounts and commissions. These funds were to be used to retire the term loan and to support future growth and expansion of the firm.

QUESTIONS

1. Discuss some advantages and disadvantages to Florida Coast Banks, Inc., of issuing convertible preferred stock instead of (a) common stock, or (b) straight debt.
2. Compute the new equity to assets ratio for Florida Coast Banks, Inc., immediately after the proceeds from the securities are received and the funds applied as indicated in the case. (*Note:* For the purposes of example, you may assume that between December 31, 1978 and the date of the application of the funds, total assets had increased by $16,125,000 and total liabilities by $15,254,000). Discuss the effect of the security issue on this ratio.
3. Make a graph (dollars versus years) showing the straight preferred value of the new issue, the call price, the expected

market value of the firm's stock, and the expected future market value of the convertible preferred. (*Note:* You may assume that the dividend yield on a similar preferred security without a conversion feature would be 11.5 per cent, that this would not change over the life of the preferred, that the funds from the new issue would have been received in September 1979, and that Florida Coast Banks, Inc., would call the security when the market value of the equivalent common stock was 20 per cent above the par value of the preferred.) Discuss your estimation of the future market value of the preferred issue.

4. Compute the pretax expected rate of return on the convertible to the investor, assuming that the common stock is sold immediately after conversion is forced.

5. (At option of the instructor.) Suppose that instead of calling the issue the firm elects to let the security remain outstanding and let investors convert when they choose. Will conversion eventually occur? Why or why not? Ignoring tax effects, when will conversion occur if it does so?

Bank of the United States

Financing with Zero-Coupon Debt

In the early 1980s, many firms and banks, faced with required bond interest rates of 14 per cent or more on new issues, were reluctant to issue the standard quarterly payment bonds with coupon rates adjusted so that such bonds would initially sell near their maturity value. Instead, many elected to issue zero-coupon bonds: instruments with no interest payments. These debt obligations were, in effect, merely promises to pay a specific amount at a specific future maturity date. Because no interest was paid in the interim, these bonds sold at a deep discount from face value, often selling initially for 30 to 50 per cent of the promised payment at maturity. The amount of this discount depended on the issue's time to maturity, the issuing firm's financial condition, and investors' expectations regarding future interest rates and inflation. Also, because there were no interim interest payments, it was expected that the future trading prices of such instruments would be extraordinarily sensitive to changes in interest rate levels.

From an individual investor's perspective, the tax treatment of these instruments was quite different from that associated with the purchase of standard interest-bearing debt at par value. Unless the purchaser was tax exempt for some reason, he or she was required to treat the annual income from the zero-coupon bond as interest and pay federal income tax on it in the year accrued, even though the money would not be received until sale or maturity. Because of this tax treatment and probably

Exhibit 38-1. BANK OF THE UNITED STATES

Details of Zero-Coupon Note Issues

Maturity Value of Issue	Maturity Value of Each Note	Initial Selling Price of Each Note	Years to Maturity
$75 million	$1,000.00	$500.00	5
$75 million	$1,000.00	$333.33	8
$50 million	$1,000.00	$250.00	10

because of their extremely volatile price prospects, zero-coupon bonds were generally marketed as instruments appropriate for tax-exempt situations in which they would be held to maturity, such as Individual Retirement Accounts or Keogh plans. From the issuing firm's standpoint, the zero-coupon issues were different from standard bonds in that they would provide cash *inflows* for profitable firms during all periods of their life except their year of maturity. This was because of the tax savings associated with the amortization of the discount on the issue.

The Bank of the United States, a publicly held firm and not a branch of the government, was one of the largest banks in the free world. In early 1982 the bank decided to issue a series of zero-coupon notes of various maturities (see Exhibit 38-1). The sale was underwritten by several large investment banking firms. In an interview in March 1982, one of the Bank of the United States' senior vice-presidents announced the details of the issue, but was not able to provide an example of the appropriate yield-to-maturity calculations because of Security and Exchange Commission regulations.

QUESTIONS

1. Calculate the yield to maturity for each of the three parts of the note issue assuming (a) that the notes are purchased by an individual investor in the 35 per cent tax bracket; and (b) that the notes are purchased by the same individual for a tax-exempt retirement plan. You may assume a linear annual income stream will be used for tax purposes.

2. Calculate the cost to maturity for the bank for each of the three parts of the note issue. You may ignore underwriting costs, assume linear discount amortization, and assume that the bank is profitable and taxed at a 46 per cent rate.

3. Contrast the net cash flows in each year and the cost to maturity from the five-year note issue with those flows and costs that the bank would have incurred had it instead decided to issue a standard 14 per cent bond of similar maturity sold initially at par. On the basis of these cash flows and costs, discuss the advantages and disadvantages of the zero-coupon instrument over the more traditional financing instrument. Which would have been of more advantage to the bank? Why?

4. (At option of the instructor.) Suppose that Congress changed the tax law to make the appreciation on the zero-coupon issue taxable at maturity at the capital gains rate rather than in the accrued periods as ordinary income. Assuming a capital gains tax rate of 20 per cent, recalculate the yield to maturity under this revised tax structure for the taxable individual. What would be the likely result of such a change on the initial selling prices of zero-coupon issues?

Natural Gas Service Company

Refunding a Long-Term Issue

The Natural Gas Service Company was a large firm located in the eastern United States. The firm in late 1979 consisted of a holding company and a series of service subsidiaries. These service subsidiaries performed various functions, including distributing natural gas along interstate pipelines, selling natural gas to consumers and businesses, and importing and distributing liquid natural gas. The firm sold gas to about 750,000 retail customers and had total sales for fiscal 1979 of one billion dollars.

The natural gas industry in the mid-1970s was under severe legislative restraint, particularly with regard to pricing. It was recognized by Congress, however, that in order to achieve energy independence by giving firms incentives to produce prices for energy sources would have to increase. Consequently, the Natural Gas Policy Act of 1978 was passed. Fiscal 1979 was the first full fiscal year for the firm during which the act was in effect. During this year, gas well completions were up 15 per cent over fiscal 1978 to set an all-time record.

Perhaps one of the firm's most interesting projects involved the importation of natural gas from overseas. In this system, which began operation in 1978, gas was produced, cooled into a liquid, and loaded on special cryogenic tanker ships in Algeria. The gas was then delivered to the firm's facilities in the United States, regasified, and distributed to users by pipeline.

Like most utilities, the firm was quite capital-intensive, and required frequent issues of new long-term financing. In early 1980, the executives of the firm wondered if it would be economical to devote part of the revenues from the firm's upcoming issue of twenty-year bonds to the retirement of the firm's 11 per cent cumulative preferred stock. This stock had been issued five years ago (in 1975) during another period of high interest rates. Although interest rates were again high (the new bonds were expected to have a 12.2 per cent coupon rate), some of the executives thought the firm might come out ahead by refunding. The provision of the preferred issue called for the preferred to be retired gradually over a period of time through a sinking fund; the average life on a preferred share then outstanding was about five years. Thus, there appeared to be two options: (1) call the preferred now and refund with bonds, or (2) refund with bonds as the preferred was called for the sinking fund.

The preferred stock then outstanding was originally issued in the face amount of $25 million; each share had a par of $100. Flotation had been 1.74 per cent of the original issue amount. If the preferred was called in early 1980 for refunding, the call price would be $112.91 per share; if it were left outstanding and called for the sinking fund, the call price would be $101.95 per share. Flotation on new bond issues was expected to be 0.58 per cent of the issue. The firm's marginal tax rate was 46 per cent.

QUESTIONS

1. Assuming that the firm issued new bonds one month before calling the preferred, calculate the initial net cash flow of an immediate refunding of the preferred stock (option 1).

2. Calculate the yearly changes in net cash flows associated with an immediate refunding compared to leaving the preferred outstanding.

3. Calculate the net present value of immediate refunding. Which option should be exercised? Why?

4. (At option of the instructor.) Discuss the impact of these other aspects of the refunding operation on the firm's decision:

   a. Considerations of optimal capital structure.

   b. Considerations regarding the timing of the refunding operation in relation to expected interest rate levels.

Xerox Corporation

Dividend Policy

Xerox Corporation was incorporated in 1906 as Haloid Company. The firm's name was changed to Haloid-Xerox, Inc. in 1958 and to Xerox Corporation in 1961. In the 1960s, the firm was considered a "high technology, growth company," having developed and marketed the first plain paper copier, the Xerox 914. This copying machine was first marketed in March 1960 and created a copying revolution. While other firms developed technologies that could also do the job, the firm's name became a synonym for copying; "to xerox" something meant to make a dry copy, regardless of the actual process used.

Into the late 1970s, the firm still retained much of its original science orientation. The cover of Xerox's 1979 annual report was a composite picture of several high-technology products, including copier parts, a cathode-ray tube computer display screen, part of a laser printer, and the control panel for a facsimile reproduction unit.

The firm in 1979 participated in many market areas besides its basic line of business. The firm had made numerous acquisitions over the years, particularly during the period from 1962 to 1979. These included educational publishing firms and computer products firms. Xerox's diverse operations included the

*This case was prepared from public information. It is designed for educational purposes, and not for research or to illustrate the correct or incorrect handling of administrative practices.

generation, manufacturing, and/or distribution of printing devices for computers, computer plotters, computer memory devices, typing systems, financial services, medical X-ray systems, reference books, and special optical systems. However, the vast bulk of the firm's operations were still centered in re-

Exhibit 40-1. XEROX CORPORATION

Consolidated Statements of Income and Balance Sheet*
(for Fiscal Year Ending 12/31/79; Millons of Dollars)

Statement of Income

Total operating revenues	$7,027.0
Total costs and expenses	5,725.7
Operating income	1,301.3
Other deductions	18.0
Income before income taxes	1,283.3
Income taxes	592.0
Income before outside shareholders' interests	691.3
Outside shareholders' interests	128.2
Net income	$ 563.1

Balance Sheet

Cash, time deposits, and marketable securities	$ 757.6
Trade receivables	1,120.4
Accrued equipment rentals due Xerox	259.3
Inventories	785.8
Other current assets	180.5
Total current assets	3,103.6
Rental equipment and related inventories	1,736.4
Land, buildings, and equipment	1,222.3
Other assets	491.3
Total assets	$6,553.6
Notes payable	96.3
Current portion of long-term debt	40.2
Accounts payable	325.1
Accruals	689.5
Income taxes	426.0
Other current liabilities	102.2
Total current liabilities	1,679.3
Long-term debt	913.0
Other long-term items	739.9
Shareholders' equity	3,221.4
Total liabilities and shareholders' equity	$6,553.6

*Source: Xerox Corporation 1979 Annual Report, pp. 35-37.

prographics: the development, manufacture, and marketing of xerographic copiers and duplicators. This basic line of business produced 75 per cent of the firm's total operating revenues for fiscal 1979 (see Exhibit 40-1 for consolidated statements of income and balance sheets for the firm). Commenting on the future direction of this business area in its 1979 annual report, the firm said, "We will continue to be a market leader in an industry which will grow at a rate faster than the Gross National Product of virtually all the countries where we operate."

The firm's profit picture continued to be very strong in 1979. Xerox's return on average assets for 1979 was 20.8 per cent, which was quite high relative to other firms. In 1979, the firm increased its cash dividends to common stock to $2.40 per share for that year, an increase of 21 per cent over 1978. This represented a dividend payout ratio for 1979 of 36 per cent of net income per common share. The firm had paid dividends to its shareholders for fifty consecutive years and had paid consecutive quarterly dividends since 1948 (see Exhibit 40-2 for some historic statistics for the firm). The firm also during 1979 significantly increased capital expenditures over the previous year. Total capital expenditures for 1979 were $1,227 million, a substantial increase over the 1978 level of $911 million. In its February 1980 meeting, the firm's board of directors again declared an increase in dividends for the first quarter, to eighty cents per share for the first quarter of 1980. This was an increase of ten cents over the firm's first quarter 1979 dividend of seventy cents per share.

QUESTIONS

1. Calculate the compounded growth rate of the firm's earnings per share, 1970 to 1979. Does the firm rate the classification "growth company" on this overall basis? Why or why not? Also calculate the compounded growth rates of earnings per share for the periods 1970 to 1974 and 1974 to 1979. Does this change your conclusion? Why or why not?

2. Calculate the firm's dividend payout ratios for the years 1970 through 1979 and the average payout ratios for the periods 1970 to 1979, 1970 to 1974, and 1975 to 1979. Discuss why Xerox might choose to increase dividends during 1979 and early 1980.

3. On the basis of the data from Question 2, is the dividend policy of Xerox consistent with the policy that you would expect from a growth firm? Discuss why it is or isn't with refer-

Exhibit 40-2. XEROX CORPORATION

Some Dividend and Other Data, Fiscal Years 1970–1979

Year	Net Income per Common Share*	Dividends per Common Share*	Average No. of Common Shares Outstanding*	Additions to Land, Bldg., and Eq.* (millions)	Reported Depreciation and Amortiza- tion (millions)
1970	$2.33	$0.65	82,361,483	$ 97	$ 34
1971	$2.58	$0.80	82,701,486	136	37
1972	$3.10	$0.84	83,203,998	131	49
1973	$3.42	$0.90	83,317,018	232	76
1974	$3.99	$1.00	83,313,252	294	102
1975	$2.98	$1.00	83,160,633	284	126
1976	$4.35	$1.10	83,923,387	214	150
1977	$4.95	$1.50	83,901,945	182	156
1978	$5.67	$2.00	84,092,274	206	163
1979	$6.69	$2.40	84,125,133	$300	$191

*Source: Xerox Corporation 1979 Annual Report, pp. 54–55.

ence to the firm's investment opportunities. You may assume that the dividend ratio for a mature firm would be 50 per cent. Are any changes in Xerox's payout ratio over time consistent with the firm's growth pattern?

4. (At option of the instructor.) Under the residual theory of dividends, the firm allocates cash flows first to the equity-financed portion of the firm's capital budget; then, if any flows remain, these are paid out in dividends. Of course, there are other uses for the money, so the cash flows from operations are not totally used for these two purposes alone. Calculate the ratios for 1970 through 1979 of dividends and capital expenditures for land, buildings, and equipment to operating cash flow and plot these data on a graph. You may use reported depreciation to approximate tax statement depreciation. Does this substantiate the idea that Xerox is using, at least as a partial consideration, elements of the residual theory in its dividend decision? Why or why not?

PART VI

Mergers and Acquisitions

F. W. Woolworth Co.*

Valuing Common Stock

As of early 1979, F. W. Woolworth was one of the largest and oldest retailers in the United States. The firm, which had been incorporated in 1911 to take over the assets and operations of prior companies, for the fiscal year ending on January 31, 1979 had domestic and foreign sales totaling more than $6 billion. According to Woolworth's 1978 annual report, the firm had seven divisions or units based on business line and geographic area: U. S. Woolworth and Woolco Division, Kinney Shoe Corporation, Richman Brothers, Woolworth and Woolco Canada, Woolworth-Germany, Woolworth-Mexico and Woolworth-Spain, and Woolworth-Great Britain. Four of these units, however, provided the majority of sales and earnings: U. S. Woolworth and Woolco Division, Kinney Shoe Corporation, Woolworth and Woolco Canada, and Woolworth-Germany. Exhibit 41-1 gives Woolworth's balance sheet as of January 31, 1979; Exhibit 41-2, Woolworth's income statement for fiscal 1978; and Exhibit 41-3, some historic data on Woolworth's income, assets, and sales.

The U. S. Woolworth and Woolco Division provided more than one half of the firm's sales volume for fiscal 1978, with a total of $3,250 million in sales. This division operated Woolworth's domestic general merchandise stores.

*This case was prepared from public information. It is designed for educational purposes and not for research or to illustrate the correct or incorrect handling of administrative practices.

Exhibit 41-1.   F. W. WOOLWORTH CO.

Consolidated Balance Sheet as of 1/31/79[1] (Thousands of Dollars)

Cash	$ 17,500
Time deposits	35,700
Trade receivables	13,800
Merchandise inventories	1,244,800
Other current assets	117,200
Total current assets	1,429,000
Investment in British subsidiary	200,300
Owned properties, less depreciation and amortization	748,900
Leased properties under capital leases, less amortization	$ 295,200
Other assets	34,100
Total assets	2,707,500
Short-term foreign debt	4,400
Long-term debt due within one year	9,300
Accounts payable	374,500
Accrued compensation and other liabilities	202,900
Dividends payable	11,200
Income taxes	75,900
Current portion of capital leases	22,000
Total current liabilities	700,200
Long-term debt	410,100
Other liabilities	44,300
Deferred income taxes	22,600
Long-term obligations under capital leases	353,500
Preferred stock[2]	8,200
Common stock[3]	97,900
Retained earnings and additional paid-in capital	1,076,200
Common stock in treasury	(5,500)
Total shareholders' equity	1,176,800
Total liabilities & owners' equity	$2,707,500

[1] Source: F. W. Woolworth Annual Report 1978, pp. 21 and 28.

[2] As of 1/31/79 there were 1,736,084 shares of this preferred stock outstanding, each convertible at a rate of 1.42 shares of common per share of preferred. During fiscal 1978, these shares generally traded between $26.75 and $32.625 per share.

[3] A total of 29,127,815 shares of this common stock were outstanding as of 1/31/79.

Kinney Shoe Corporation had been acquired by Woolworth in 1963 from Brown Shoe Company. Kinney operated the Kinney shoe chain, Susie's Casuals (a rapidly growing women's apparel chain), and Foot Locker (an athletic footwear and

Exhibit 41-2.   F. W. WOOLWORTH CO.

Consolidated Statement of Income for Fiscal 1978[1]
(Thousands of Dollars)

Sales and other income	$6,117,100
Cost of sales	4,268,500
Selling, administration, and general expenses	1,483,800
Depreciation and amortization	77,300
Interest on borrowings	59,900
Income before income taxes	227,600
Income taxes	122,700
Income of consolidated companies	104,900
Equity in net income of British subsidiary	25,400
Net income	$ 130,300

[1] Source: F. W. Woolworth Annual Report 1978, page 20.

apparel chain) in the United States, Canada, and Australia. In fiscal 1978, total sales for this unit were $808 million.

Woolworth maintained a substantial position in Canadian retailing through the firm's Woolworth and Woolco Canada unit, with sales in fiscal 1978 of $1,147 million (U. S. dollars). The unit operated 315 Woolworth and Woolco stores and was planning to open eleven more in 1979.

Woolworth-Germany operated 199 stores in West Germany. Sales reached $743 million for this unit for fiscal 1978, but this 28 per cent increase from the previous year was partly caused by appreciation of the German mark against the U. S. dollar. In local currency, sales had increased only 11 per cent.

Although Woolworth was a sizable retailing firm, it was not unknown for U. S. firms of this type to be acquisition targets for foreign firms in the late 1970s. During this period, the Agache-Willot Group, a diversified French firm, had acquired Korvettes Inc., a U. S. department store chain. Tootal Ltd., a British firm, had acquired Ups 'n Downs, a U. S. chain of women's clothing shops. This pattern of acquisitions may have been facilitated by the impression that the common stocks of U. S. firms were undervalued. During 1978, Woolworth's stock generally traded between $17.125 and $23 per share; for fiscal 1978, the firm earned $4.34 per share diluted for stock option plans ($4.12 fully diluted to include convertible preferred stock). On April 9, 1979, with Woolworth's stock trading at $26 per share, Brascan Ltd. made a tender offer to Woolworth's shareholders of $35 per common share, an offer totaling $1.13 billion in U. S. dollars.

Exhibit 41-3.   F. W. WOOLWORTH CO.

Historic Data on Dividends, Earnings per Share, Sales, and Total Assets[1]

Fiscal Year	1978	1977	1976	1975	1974	1973	1972	1971	1970
Dividend/share	1.40	1.40	1.25	1.20	1.20	1.20	1.20	1.20	1.20
Earnings/share (primary)	4.34	2.81	3.61	3.40	1.76	3.14	2.66	2.63	2.29
Earnings/share (fully diluted)	4.12	2.71	3.45	3.26	1.74	3.02	2.57	2.51	2.24
Sales (rounded millions)	6,103	5,535	5,152	4,650	4,177	3,722	3,119	3,148	2,801
Total assets (millions)	2,707	2,465	2,376	2,459	2,343	1,974	N. A.	1,720	1,580

[1] Sources: Figures from 1974–1978 from F. W. Woolworth Company Annual Report 1978; prior figures from Moody's Industrial Manuals. Figures from 1974–1978 reflect capitalization of lease expense; prior years do not.

Brascan Ltd. was a Canadian firm which, through subsidiaries, was engaged in real estate, consumer and industrial services, natural resources, and financial services in Canada and Brazil. Brascan's holdings included 68 per cent of Triarch Corporation (a Canadian investment banking firm), 100 per cent of Brascan Resources Ltd. (a Canadian natural resources exploration and development firm), 24 per cent of London Life Insurance Company (a Canadian life insurance firm), 51 per cent of Western Mines Ltd. (a Canadian mining firm), and 24 per cent of John Labatt Ltd. (a diversified brewer), as well as other interests. The firm, founded in Brazil in 1912, had begun a major diversification program in the late 1960s. Before its tender offer for Woolworth's stock, Brascan had quite a bit of cash on hand, having just sold its 83 per cent interest in a Brazilian electric utility for $380 million. Brascan's offer to buy the stock of Woolworth may have been in part a defensive move to prevent its own acquisition; Edper Equities Ltd. of Toronto had announced that it was considering a tender offer to holders of Brascan shares.

Woolworth's board of directors opposed the tender offer by Brascan, claiming in part that the offer of $35 per share was inadequate. A stockholder then sued Woolworth and its board to enjoin them from blocking the proposed tender offer. Amid legal and other controversies, Brascan later withdrew and abandoned its offer for Woolworth.

QUESTIONS

1. Calculate the common shareholder's book equity per share for F. W. Woolworth based on full dilution as of January 31, 1979. You may assume that stock options totaling 800,000 shares are outstanding.

2. Assume that a reasonable price/earnings ratio for Woolworth on the basis of economic conditions in early 1979 would have been 8.0. According to fiscal 1978 earnings, calculate a value per common share.

3. Using the perpetual-growth, dividend-capitalization model and assuming a stockholder's required return of 13 per cent per year, calculate an equilibrium price per common share of Woolworth as of early 1979. Justify any assumptions you may make regarding the growth rate of future dividends.

4. Contrast the three share values obtained in Questions 1 to 3 with the $35 per share offer by Brascan. Was the offer fair to Woolworth's shareholders according to this comparison?

5. (At option of the instructor.) Why might the management of a firm want to resist a tender offer of this type, even though it was higher than the current market price of shares and would have increased shareholder wealth?

6. (At option of the instructor.) Assess Brascan's offer in light of current research on market efficiency.

Cutter Laboratories, Inc.

*Valuing the Distressed Firm**

Cutter Laboratories, Inc. was a producer of medical and other products, including human biologicals, allergy products, hospital products, human plasma solutions, veterinary products, plastic products, and prosthetic heart and knuckle devices. The company had experienced significant growth in the years 1962 to 1971 in total assets, tangible net worth per share, earnings per share, and sales (the firm's balance sheets and income statements for fiscals 1962–1972 are presented in Exhibit 42-1). The firm sold products in domestic and foreign markets.

The firm in 1972 had two classes of common stock outstanding: class A and class B. Each class of stock was entitled to one vote per share; voting separately, each class elected one half of the directors. Class A stock had the right of cumulative voting for directors; otherwise, the rights and privileges of the two classes were the same. Dividends had been paid on the currently outstanding stock and on prior classes of common in every year since 1947. The firm's stock was traded on the American Stock Exchange and listed on the Pacific Stock Exchange.

Despite seemingly bright prospects, in late 1972 the firm began to have difficulties with its products. In early October, the firm announced that it had temporarily stopped producing and distributing irrigating solutions in screw-top containers because

*This case was prepared from public information. It is designed for educational purposes and not for research or to illustrate the correct or incorrect handling of administrative practices.

Exhibit 42-1. CUTTER LABORATORIES, INC.

Consolidated Balance Sheets and Statements of Income for Fiscal Years Ending 12/31/62 to 12/31/72
(Ordered by the Accountant's Method; in Rounded Thousands of Dollars)

Year	1972	1971	1970	1969	1968	1967	1966	1965	1964	1963	1962
Cash and sec.	$ 2,494	$ 6,386	$ 201	$ 901	$ 421	$ 867	$ 2,325	$ 3,473	$ 3,114	$ 2,632	$ 1,455
Accts. rec.	13,310	12,814	12,439	9,354	7,900	6,711	6,258	5,552	4,598	4,107	5,462
Inventories	38,094	29,077	22,801	20,588	16,476	13,755	11,351	8,809	9,010	9,328	8,201
Other CA	3,298	1,477	1,050	1,243	1,076	925	499	434	443	463	367
Total CA	57,197	49,755	36,491	32,085	25,872	22,258	20,434	18,268	17,164	16,531	15,484
Net property	27,349	23,150	17,149	16,095	14,470	11,686	8,460	7,367	6,741	5,227	5,340
Other assets	1,318	1,162	889	1,523	1,575	1,472	482	472	529	417	413
Intangibles	813	818	823	828	833	838	836	772	779	—	—
	86,677	74,885	55,682	50,430	42,649	36,255	30,212	26,879	25,113	22,175	21,237
Accts. pay.	4,329	4,312	3,761	3,526	2,949	3,284	2,701	2,015	1,893	1,964	1,921
Notes pay.	957	1,008	64	77	1,377	4,436	310	310	370	—	—
Dividends pay.	283	280	229	227	226	225	183	141	140	87	—
Accruals	3,440	3,960	2,648	2,353	1,867	1,662	1,774	1,451	1,473	1,267	1,140
Income taxes	751	2,581	1,118	820	539	511	1,716	1,446	843	1,074	1,104
Total CL	9,760	12,141	7,820	7,002	6,958	10,118	6,684	5,363	4,719	4,390	4,165

Notes pay.	26,841	14,695	20,123	18,487	12,864	4,935	5,070	5,380	5,159	5,000	5,000
Def. taxes	1,801	1,176	869	691	392	237	—	—	—	—	—
Pref. stk.	—	—	—	—	—	—	—	—	600	650	1,100
Class A com.	2,071	2,060	1,589	1,570	1,550	1,540	1,527	1,513	1,495	1,260	1,243
Class B com.	497	505	505	505	505	505	505	505	532	532	532
Paid in surp.	23,119	22,685	6,378	6,025	5,635	5,437	5,176	4,988	4,731	3,960	3,827
Ret. earns.	22,588	21,623	18,398	16,151	14,744	13,482	11,251	9,130	7,878	6,382	5,370
Total lia. and equity	$86,677	$74,885	$55,682	$50,430	$42,649	$36,255	$30,212	$26,879	$25,113	$22,175	$21,237
Tangible net worth per common share	$18.50	$18.38	$12.45	$11.38	$10.52	$9.84	$8.69	$7.95	$6.87	$6.77	$6.18

Par value of both classes of common stock is $1 per share.

Net sales	89,205	86,484	70,349	59,476	51,430	48,652	44,474	38,382	36,406	32,238	29,934
Cost of sales	57,267	50,656	40,646	33,354	28,601	26,044	23,688	20,414	18,998	17,205	16,200
Selling exp.	27,772	26,902	23,250	20,462	17,882	16,807	15,390	14,164	13,742	12,171	11,068
Interest exp.	1,220	1,076	1,461	1,132	871	374	292	312	303	301	315
Income taxes	855	3,556	2,352	2,214	1,910	2,336	2,295	1,668	1,449	1,171	1,208
Extraordinary credit	—	—	361	—	—	—	—	—	—	—	—
Net income	2,091	4,294	3,001	2,314	2,165	3,090	2,809	1,823	1,684	1,391	1,144
Common divs.	1,126	1,069	912	907	902	858	689	562	438	346	89
Pref. divs. and other charges			(158)					8	(250)	33	54
Additions to ret. earns.	965	3,225	2,247	1,407	1,262	2,232	2,120	1,253	1,496	1,012	1,002
Net income per common share	$0.82	$1.84	$1.45	$1.12	$1.05	$1.51	$1.39	$0.90	$0.83	$0.78	$0.62
Dividends per common share	$0.44	$0.44	$0.44	$0.44	$0.44	$0.40	$0.32	$0.28	$0.22	$0.15	$0.05

too many of these products were failing the firm's sterility tests. Irrigating solutions must be germ-free because they are used to clean and treat wounds (among other things). Nearly all of the irrigating solutions produced by the firm were packaged in screw-top containers. Sales of these solutions accounted for less than 5 per cent of the firm's revenue. In early December, Cutter announced that it was testing a modified version of the manufacturing process for these solutions and that regular production of irrigating solutions would begin shortly after test runs proved the success of the modified process. Problems associated with the irrigating solutions were expected to cost the firm twenty-five cents per share in earnings.

The company in March 1973 announced the voluntary recall of some bottles of one of its intravenous solutions. Intravenous solutions are introduced directly into the bloodstream and must be sterile. Three women in a Milwaukee hospital had developed serious infections after surgery and one woman had died. A possible cause was the intravenous solution used. Although the recall eventually involved only part of one lot of an intravenous solution produced in Cutter's Chattanooga, Tennessee plant, the recall was broadened to include additional lots later in the month; bacterial contamination was suspected. In early April, the firm recalled all the injection solutions made at this plant and announced that this would probably result in a consolidated net loss in 1973. Trading in Cutter's common stock was suspended in the morning of the day of this announcement but was reopened in the afternoon; the class A stock closed at $6.75 per share, down $2.25 for the day; the class B stock closed at $7.00, down $2.625. About thirty-two different products were involved in the recall and production stoppage, although production of similar products continued at the firm's Ogden, Utah plant. By mid-April, three deaths and several other cases of illness had possibly been linked to the intravenous solution originally recalled.

In late April, the firm suspended its dividend and delayed its first quarter earnings report. In mid-May, when the first quarter results were finally announced, a $7.4 million net loss was reported, including a $10.5 million dollar charge associated with the injection solutions recall. In late July, the firm reported a net loss for the second quarter of $1.5 million. Losses were again reported in the third quarter; total losses for the first three quarters of 1973 were $9.8 million. During the period when recalls and losses were announced, the price of the firm's stock had declined severely.

In October and November of 1973 the Cutter story took a new turn: Cutter became an acquisition target. First, officials of Cutter and Akzona Inc. (a manufacturer of fibers, pharmaceuticals, electronic products, and chemicals) announced that the companies were exploring the possibility of Akzona acquiring Cutter. In late November, trading in Cutter's common stock was suspended at Cutter's request while the firm's directors considered offers for the firm. On November 26, before the halt, the class A common closed at $13.125 (up twelve and a half cents) and the class B common, at $13.00 (up thirty-seven and a half cents). A few days later, with trading in the stock still suspended, Cutter announced that Rhinechem Corporation, a U.S. subsidiary of a German chemical firm, had indicated it planned a cash tender offer of $18.50 per share for all class A and B common shares of Cutter. About 2.6 million shares of stock were outstanding; about 450,000 shares were held by the Cutter family. Certain members of the family, including Edward A. Cutter, Jr., chairman of the firm's board and David Cutter, president, indicated they would tender their shares once the offer was made. In early January, Rhinechem announced the success of the tender offer; as of December 28, about 94 per cent of the outstanding class A shares and 88 per cent of the class B shares had already been tendered, although the offer had been extended until January 18.

QUESTIONS

1. The basic issue of the case is what was the value of the equity of Cutter Laboratories, Inc. as of late 1973? What should Rhinechem have paid for it? As of September 1973, compute (a) the value of the firm's equity if the firm was liquidated; (b) the market value of the firm's equity; (c) the book value of the firm's equity; and (d) the value of the firm's equity on the basis of the dividend capitalization model. You may assume that the firm's losses in the first three quarters of 1973 were financed by increasing debt; that assets as of September 30, 1973 were the same as December 31, 1972; and that cash and securities could be liquidated at 100 per cent of book value, current assets other than these at 60 per cent of book value, and property at 45 per cent of book value.

2. Why is the dividend capitalization model not a very appropriate one for estimating the stock value in this case?

3. What other factors may have influenced the price chosen

for Rhinechem's tender offer? (Rhinechem's parent firm made pharmaceuticals in Europe but had no U. S. medical products capacity.)

4. Evaluate the price chosen for Rhinechem's tender offer. Do you think it paid more than fair value in order to obtain the stock of the firm? Why or why not? From what do you think its offer was derived?

5. (At option of the instructor.) Taking into account the current state of research on stock market efficiency, discuss the value of the equity of Cutter Laboratories, Inc. Discuss other ways in which Rhinechem could have obtained control of Cutter.

PART VII

Bankruptcy, Reorganization, and Liquidation

Central Virginia Molders, Inc.

The Ins and Outs of a Bankruptcy

In March 1973, Eric Jones, the assistant credit manager of a manufacturer of plastic materials, had the unhappy duty of attending a bankruptcy proceeding at a bankruptcy court in Virginia. Six months previously, Jones had approved an initial shipment with an invoice value of $7,000 to Central Virginia Molders, Inc. and no payment had been made on the account; Central Virginia Molders had declared bankruptcy in January. Jones' firm was now one of the unsecured creditors in the bankruptcy proceeding.

Jones' decision to grant unsecured credit to Central Virginia Molders, Inc. had been based to a great extent on the financial statements of the firm, which had been forwarded to him by the firm's salesman to the account. This had made Jones somewhat suspicious, because he knew that firms who did not send their financial statements through the mails sometimes had something to hide. Firms using false financial statements to present a picture of inflated credit worthiness knew that sendind such statements through the mails constituted use of the mail to defraud, a federal crime, whereas only the lesser crime of fraud applied if these statements were not mailed. However, creditworthy firms also commonly presented statements to salesmen on the grounds that they were proud of their financial position and did not consider the figures to be confidential. In making the credit-granting decision, Jones had computed the current, quick, and total debt to total assets ratios for Central

Virginia Molders and found these to be 0.89, 0.55, and 0.83 for the most recent fiscal year-end. These were below the industry averages, which for firms of this size, class, and business line were 1.50, 0.80, and 0.60, respectively. From a creditor's standpoint Jones considered the firm's financial position adequate. (The latest financial figures available to Jones at the time of his credit decision are presented in Exhibit 43-1.)

Exhibit 43-1. CENTRAL VIRGINIA MOLDERS, INC.

Financial Statements as of June 30, 1972 (Unaudited)

Balance Sheet as of June 30, 1972 (Rounded Thousands of Dollars)

Cash	$ 23	Due to banks short-term*	$ 58
Accts. receivable	115	Due to trade	109
Inventory	88	Other current liabilities	94
Other current assets	5	Total current liabilities	$261
Total current assets	$231		
		Due to banks long-term*	238
Net fixed assets	368	Net worth	100
Total assets	$599	Total liab. and N.W.	$599

*Bank borrowings are unsecured.

Income Statement for Fiscal Year Ending
June 30, 1972 (Rounded Thousands of Dollars)

Sales	$1,193
Cost of sales	888
Selling and other expenses	283
Earnings before taxes	22
Income taxes	7
Earnings after taxes	$ 15

Since his firm had shipped the $7,000 worth of material, Jones had discovered that the financial statements presented to him were not those of Central Virginia Molders, Inc. alone. The statements were, in fact, consolidated statements of Central Virginia Molders, Inc. and BBB Tools Corporation. The owner and manager of the plastics molding operation, Roscoe West, had set up two corporations: BBB Tools, which was the holder of the physical assets (the molding machines and the building), and Central Virginia Molders, which held the paper, current, and cash assets (accounts receivable and inventory), incurred all the debts and transacted all the real business of the operation.

Thus, creditors' claims would not be against any of the firm's long-term assets.

Upon entering the room where the initial proceedings were to be conducted, Jones noticed that most of the local creditors were accompanied by their attorneys. This struck him as odd, because he knew that attorneys were not usually necessary at such proceedings. The Bankruptcy Judge, after arriving late announced that she had not slept the previous night and that her daughter-in-law had just had a baby girl. The local lawyers then rose and applauded. The judge, an attorney herself, then proceeded to criticize those creditors who had not been accompanied by attorneys for offending the dignity of the court.

Roscoe West then went to the front of the room and was examined by his attorney. West claimed that he could repay creditors within six months if the economy improved and if he could get a Small Business Administration (SBA) loan. At this point one of the local creditors had some quarrel with the proceedings and the Judge retired to her chambers to discuss the matter. This gave Jones a chance to discuss the bankruptcy with the other creditors.

Like Jones, they shared some serious doubts as to whether the plans outlined by West could work. The economy showed no sign of an upturn and West reportedly had been trying to get a SBA loan for some time without success. Further, rumors were that his production controls were extremely poor and the firm was having difficulty getting work.

The proceedings did not last long after the Judge returned. The creditors were allowed to ask a few questions, although questions from those not represented by attorneys were discouraged or disallowed by the Judge. West was instructed to submit to the court within six months more specific plans for reorganization and repayment.

Nothing seemingly happened for the next eighteen months. Jones periodically called the office of the Bankruptcy Judge, only to be told that a specific plan had not been filed and that no proceedings were scheduled. About one and a half years after the initial proceedings, Jones received a notice from the court that Central Virginia Molders, Inc. was to be liquidated rather than reorganized. The next month, the assets of Central Virginia Molders, Inc. were sold to BBB Tools Corporation for $10,000. This figure was just less than the court fees associated with the bankruptcy, so no money was left for any creditors. Jones wondered if it would not have been more in the creditors' interest if the firm had been liquidated initially, rather than giving West another year and a half to deplete the firm's assets.

QUESTIONS

1. Did each of the ratios calculated by Jones correctly portray the credit worthiness of the creditor firm? Why or why not? If not, recalculate and interpret any misspecified ratios.

2. Compute the liquidation value in dollars of Central Virginia Molders, Inc. as of March 1973. You may assume that the firm is in the same financial position as on June 30, 1972 and that the following recovery percents apply:

Asset	Liquidation Recovery (Percent of Book Value)
Cash and marketable securities	100
Accounts receivable	70
Inventories	70
Prepaid expenses	70
Long-term physical assets	50
All questionable assets	0

Assuming that this is the approximate liquidation value of the firm as of the time of the bankruptcy filing and that priority claims (bankruptcy expenses) would total about $13,000, compute the per cent recovery for creditors if the firm had been liquidated immediately.

3. It is sometimes said that bankruptcy proceedings are at least partially to protect creditors' interests. Does this seem to have occurred in this case? Why or why not?

4. Was there anything Jones could have done to increase his firm's recovery? Explain your answer.

5. (At option of the instructor.) Why did West set up the business organization of his operation as he did? Is this a common practice? Give one advantage and one disadvantage inherent in this system of legal organization.

L and S Manufacturing Company

Reorganization/Liquidation Decisions:
Creditor's View

L and S Manufacturing Company was a general manufacturer of metal parts, located in Philadelphia, Pennsylvania. The firm had been started in the mid-1950s by Larry and Sidney Magee, two machinists. It had grown over the years and had reached substantial size, with sales of about $3.1 million for fiscal 1979 (financial statements for the firm are presented in Exhibits 44-1 and 44-2). The firm's stock was traded locally, although the Magee family still held a controlling interest. However, high interest rates, occasional economic slowdowns, and substantial competition from other metal parts manufacturers had caused a deterioration in the firm's profitability and liquidity during the 1970s. In early 1980, the firm found itself uanble to satisfy creditors and filed a bankruptcy petition, intending to reorganize the debt structure of the firm.

Had the firm filed this petition several months earlier, management would have had to choose under which "chapter" of the federal Bankruptcy Act the firm wished to initiate proceedings. Under Chapter 11 of this act, management would have remained in control of the company and worked out its own reorganization plan. This plan would have had to be approved by each class of creditors on two votes: simple majority and dollars owed. Under Chapter 10, a trustee would have been appointed by the court to develop such a plan (rather than management), but the approval vote would have been similar. If it was found that reorganization was not possible, then the

Exhibit 44-1. L AND S MANUFACTURING COMPANY

Balance Sheets for 12/31/78 and 12/31/79 (Ordered by
the Accountant's Method)

	12/31/79	12/31/78
Cash	$ 528	$ 0
Accounts receivable, Trade	661,253	468,280
Officers	14,768	414
Other	8,953	115,191
Inventories	566,411	536,136
Prepaid expenses	13,675	14,566
Tax claim receivable	0	36,184
Total current assets	1,265,588	1,170,771
Investment in subsidiary[1]	210,865	210,865
Property, plant, and equipment net of depreciation	619,794	475,368
Other assets[2]	312,399	324,610
Total assets	2,408,646	2,181,614
Notes payable, bank[3]	203,984	157,399
Current portion LTD[3]	74,344	63,473
Accounts payable, trade	960,292	679,790
Accruals	272,755	317,248
Total current liabilities	1,511,375	1,217,910
Long-term debt[3]	503,160	576,939
Preferred stock	44,970	44,970
Common stock	87,240	87,240
Additional paid-in capital	360,184	360,184
Retained earnings	(98,283)	(105,629)
Net worth of common	349,141	341,795
Total liabilities and net worth	$2,408,646	$2,181,614

[1] Investment in subsidiary is at cost. As of 12/31/79, the net worth of the subsidiary was $(23,736).
[2] Other assets include proposal engineering costs and product development costs.
[3] Notes due to bank and long-term debt are secured by trade accounts receivable and inventory.

firm could be liquidated. This was exactly what had occurred in the bankruptcy of the W. T. Grant retail chain.

This system was adequate but involved time-consuming problems as to which chapter was proper for a particular firm. Because the Bankruptcy Court could move petitioners from one chapter into another, there were often legal disputes in which substantial time and money were expended. The bankrupt's

Exhibit 44-2.   L AND S MANUFACTURING COMPANY

Statements of Income and Retained Earnings for Fiscal
Years Ending 12/31/78 and 12/31/79 (Ordered by the
Accountant's Method)

	12/31/79	12/31/78
Sales	$3,084,655	$2,486,849
Cost of sales	2,672,355	2,235,071
Gross margin on sales	412,300	251,778
Selling, administrative and general expenses	433,441	364,763
Operating income	(21,141)	(112,985)
Other income	31,211	16,045
Other expenses	0	0
Profit before taxes	10,070	(96,940)
Taxes	2,724	0
Income after taxes	7,346	(96,940)
Ret. earnings, beginning of year	(105,629)	(8,689)
Ret. earnings, end of year	$ (98,283)	$ (105,629)

management often wanted to remain in control, but creditors
sometimes believed that the firm would be run more in their
interests by a trustee. To avoid such problems, Congress passed
legislation in late 1978, effective October 1, 1979, combining
Chapters 10 and 11. Under this new system, management would
stay in control unless there was shown to be cause (such as
fraud, incompetence, or gross mismanagement) for a trustee to
be appointed, or unless the court believed that such an appointment would be in the best interests of creditors and stockholders.

Sam Manges, general credit manager of Spare Parts Distributors, was well aware of these statutes and their application to
the L and S Manufacturing situation. L and S had petitioned the
courts for protection under the new bankruptcy statutes several
months ago, and at the time had owed Spare Parts Distributors
about $20,000. Manges was trying to decide how to vote on
the reorganization plan that had been proposed by the management of L and S. The firm had stated that should the plan not
be passed by creditors, the firm would probably be liquidated.

For the class of creditors into which Spare Parts Distributors
fell, the plan provided for an immediate cash payout of five
cents for each dollar owed. This payout was to be funded by a
capital contribution from the Magee family, for which they
would receive additional common stock. Creditors in the class
would also receive shares of a new class of preferred stock at a

rate of thirty-five cents in par value for each dollar owed. This stock would pay a 2 per cent (based on par value) cash dividend during each year that it was outstanding and would be redeemed on a random basis at par value over the next ten years; thus, the expected outstanding period on this new preferred would be five years. The remaining sixty cents owed would be a write-off for creditors against their reserves for bad debt.

Manges noted that L and S had no subordinated debt. If the firm went into liquidation, the firm's assets would be sold and the proceeds distributed. Manges expected this procedure to take about a year. Proceeds would go first to "priority claims" (administrative expenses of the bankruptcy, taxes, and wages.) Secured creditors, of course, would receive the proceeds from the sale of the specific secured property. Any excess money from the sale of secured properties after secured creditors were paid would revert to other creditors. Likewise, if money from the sale of secured property was insufficient to pay secured creditors in full, their remaining debts would be included with general creditors. Should funds be sufficient to completely satisfy general creditors also, funds would be available for stockholders. Spare Parts Distributors was a general creditor of L and S.

Manges had experience in several liquidation situations and was aware that the liquidation value, or value in forced sale, of the firm's assets was not the same as the book value, and also usually varied from asset to asset and firm to firm according to the type and quality of asset and the firm's line of business. In general, he had found the following estimated recovery per-cents to be useful guidelines:

Asset	Recovery as a Percent of Book Value
Cash	100%
Marketable securities	Current Market Value
Accounts receivable	70%
Inventory	~~70%~~ 55%
Prepaid expenses	70%
All long-term assets	50%
All questionable assets	0%

On the basis of his experience with the metal parts industry, Manges had decided to reduce the expected per cent recovery on inventory from 70 per cent to 55 per cent. He also knew that these estimated per cents were merely guesses and that actual recoveries might vary considerably from his estimates.

QUESTIONS

1. Calculate the expected net cash flows to Spare Parts Distributors in each period from the plan of reorganization proposed by the management of L and S.

2. Calculate the net present value to Spare Parts Distributors of the plan of reorganization. Justify the discount rates used based on the riskiness of various cash flows.

3. Calculate the expected recovery in dollars of Spare Parts Distributors if L and S should liquidate. You may assume that the firm's financial position at the time of liquidation would be about the same as that as of December 31, 1979 and that priority claims would total $100,000, $50,000 of which was included in accruals as of 12/31/79. State any other assumptions. Justify the discount rate used.

4. What should Manges do? Why?

5. (At option of the instructor.) One of the assumptions of the Modigliani and Miller propositions of capital structure is that there are no bankruptcy costs. That is, the assumption is that the firm incurs no material additional expenses because of bankruptcy and that assets are liquidated at their market values. Discuss the validity of this assumption in light of Manges' experiences regarding liquidations of firms in bankruptcy. What are the implications of your conclusions for Modigliani and Miller's Proposition I with taxes?